RESPONSES

CW015...

0 0 1 6 2 8

Nelson

█ R E S P O N S E S █

Series editors: Angel and Patrick Scott

Community Writing by Don Shiach
Frankie Mae and other stories by Ann Mann and Hilary Rich
Wordlife by Richard Knott
In the event by Roger Samways

Editors' note
GCSE reflects the most interesting and successful initiatives in
English teaching that have taken place over the last 15 to 20 years.
As a consequence it is no longer possible to ignore classroom talk,
or to pretend that 'response' doesn't play an important part in
reading, and 'variety' in writing. No longer can the English curriculum
be sliced up into lessons on 'comprehension' or 'essay writing' or
'spelling'; the constituent parts of the subject are 'clearly inter-related
and interdependent' (National Criteria for GCSE), and one activity has
to grow naturally out of another.

This series builds on these principles. It aims to make available for
pupils some of the best contemporary sources ranging from familiar
literary genres, like poetry or the short story, to less conventional
forms, like community writing. The 'follow-on' work that is included at
the back of each book suggests ways in which teachers might use
the material to provoke discussion, develop ideas for folios of work
and introduce pupils to new ways of reading texts. That is why the
series as a whole is called '*Responses*'.

Angel and Patrick Scott

■ CONTENTS ■

■ INTRODUCTION ■

This anthology is a collection of personal and autobiographical writing, short stories and poetry by non-professional authors from many different parts of the country and from various cultural backgrounds. The individual pieces were chosen from among the many publications that writers' groups and writing projects have produced over the last few years.

This book is intended primarily to help pupils prepare for the GCSE English examination by providing accessible models for their own writing. The authors' ages range from the teenager to the elderly. All the writing has a direct appeal to readers because of its freshness of approach and uncluttered clarity.

One of the anthologies from which the contents of this book were chosen has the title, 'If you can talk, you can write'. I would certainly agree with the underlying belief behind this statement: we are all potential writers. Writing does not belong exclusively to the professionals or the 'great' writers. We all have something in our lives to write about because we all share experience and live in communities. However, to communicate well through our writing, we have to learn something of the craft of writing. The contents of this book should help pupils to learn something of that craft and to apply it to their own writing.

Don Shiach 1987

Keeping a personal record

The first section consists of nine pieces written in the first person. Each of these writers has tried to describe an important experience in his or her life. They are attempting to put into words a truthful and accurate record of personal experience. The very act of writing about it perhaps makes that experience more enduring and significant. Writing about the experience clarifies something essential about it and is an attempt to communicate this to the reader.

■ It was really great when ■ Jaye was born

The Monday night before the baby was born, this very strange, violent kicking started just as we got into bed. I turned to John and said, 'Do you think this baby is trying to tell us something?' We both laughed about it, thinking what a mad idea. I tossed and turned quite a bit as it was very hard by now to get comfortable before falling asleep. Suddenly it was 5 a.m. I had woken up because I started feeling a pain. I went to the loo, but the pain still kept coming. It was very cold in the flat. I looked out of the front room window to find – fourteen floors down – there was snow on the ground and snow still falling. So I turned the heating on full and then started to walk the flat every ten minutes.

My cat must have thought I had gone mad as she chased me up and down the hall, then back into the front room. When the pain was bad I felt better if I walked about, but as it faded I rested on the sofa.

This all went on for about an hour. By the time 6 a.m. had gone, the pains were definitely coming every ten minutes, so I thought I had better wake John. To my suprise, he jumped out of bed straightaway, saying, 'Why didn't you wake me at five, Sue?' I asked him if he wanted tea. He said, 'There's no time for tea, I've got to phone the hospital straightaway.' He was gone for about twenty minutes.

I was all packed and ready to go. We met the ambulance men down at the entrance to our flats about ten minutes to seven. They were two young blokes and straightaway made a joke about it snowing and how they always get an expectant mum just as they are finishing their shift for the night. Because they were there, I tried to be brave and just laugh along with them, but the pain

4

was a lot sharper now.

Because I was sitting down now, when the pain did come it made me jump. Inside I was nervous about getting to the hospital. But all I had to do when we got there was just to sit in a wheelchair and wait. I had to wait for the day porters to come as the night shift had just finished and it made me feel really funny because wheelchairs are for invalids and I didn't feel like one.

It must have been about 8 a.m. by the time we actually arrived at the maternity ward. I was taken to a small sort of waiting room. By this time, I began to feel rather sick at the thought of the whole thing. It was such a comfort to me that John was there. About 8.30, a doctor came and felt my stomach and listened to the baby. He said all was fine, and that a midwife nurse would come to see me again soon. The pain was now every two minutes. At 9 a.m. I was moved to another room, where I had an internal examination. The midwife decided that the baby was well ready to be born.

Then I was moved into the actual delivery room, and John came with me. I was asked if I needed any of the different painkillers, such as an epidural or pethidine injection. I had talked to John about this earlier while we were waiting and I decided I had taken the pain up till now without painkillers, so I just had the gas and air. John controlled this for me in the delivery room, making sure I didn't get much of a look-in because it is dangerous to take too much at once.

By the time the doctor and nurses were ready, it was about 9.30 a.m. and this is when things really got going. The long, hard slog began of pushing and breathing, making sure it was co-ordinating with the pain. John had his hand on the back of my neck which helped me to push, as well as being a lot of support emotionally. It was a nice, cosy room, not too bright or clinical looking. Everyone in the room rallied round to encourage me to push.

It was 11 a.m. now. Still no baby. The doctor in charge told us I was going to have a forceps birth. Afterwards I would be stitched. By this time I was only too pleased to get help. It was all too late for those painkillers now. The doctor in charge asked if John wanted to stay during the forceps delivery. He said he wanted to. This was really good because some doctors don't like the father present because it makes them nervous. My legs were put up into stirrups which was weird, very undignified. By this time I really needed the gas. It was just so great that I had John with me. I don't know how he stayed through the birth.

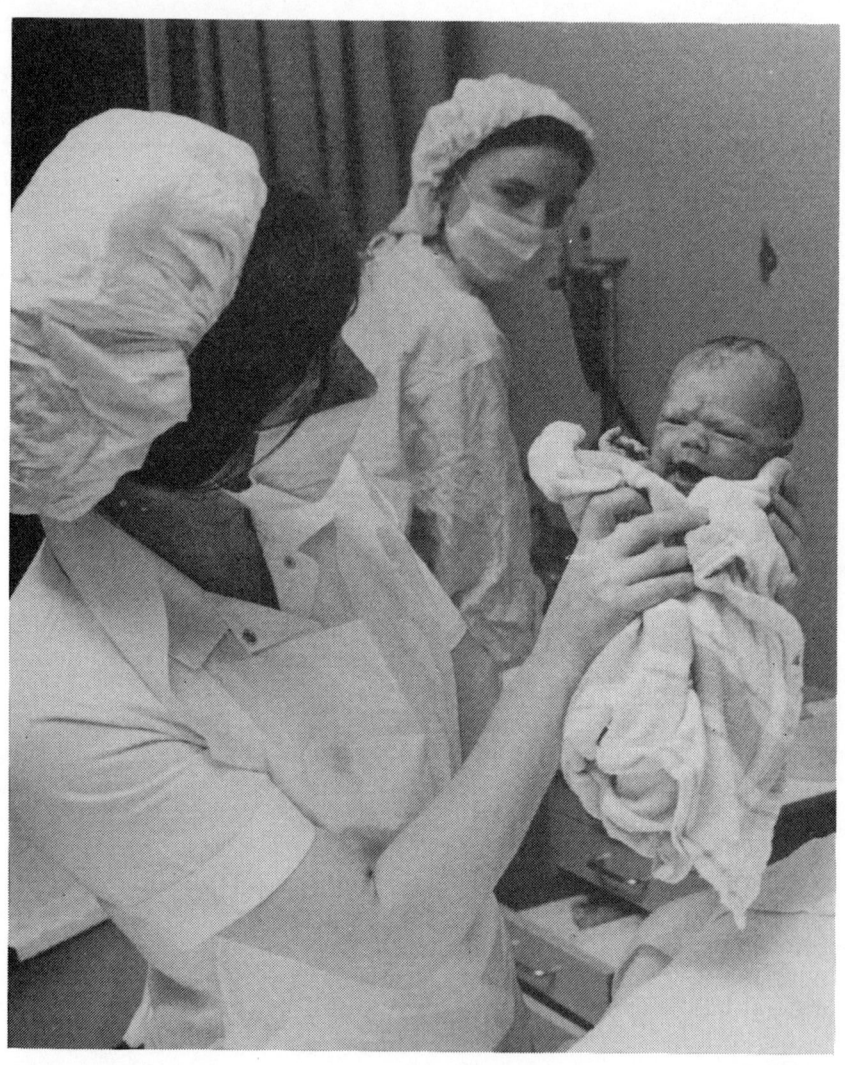

It was really great when Jaye was born. Once the doctor had pulled her out I heard him say, 'It's a girl.' John's face was really happy.

They laid her on my stomach straightaway. It was amazing. Her eyes were wide open and as John reached to touch her, her little fingers curled round his. We were so happy, you just can't believe it. To think yesterday she was in my stomach and today she's outside alive and kicking.

Suzanne Bissmire

■ The boy ■

My earliest memories always centre or focus on a period during my childhood.

From birth to fourteen years old I lived in a small, mainly farming, village community. My father worked a few miles away during sugar-cane harvesting. My mother stayed home to look after us children. She occasionally visited my grandmother who lived several miles away. She also went to market with vegetables which were grown collectively on my grandmother's small 'farm'. The money she received for the sale of food surplus to the family's needs was used to buy 'dry goods', and treats.

My father bought a new clock and placed it reverently on the wall. I was fascinated by this 'super' toy. Every evening my father would wind the clock and I made sure I was always present. One evening, wanting to be proud and manly in my Dad's eyes, I decided to wind it, partly to satisfy my own curiosity and also to be a clever boy: 'Look what I've done'. On climbing down, I fell and broke the clock. At this point the hand began a demented race against time. My father's rage and the painful aftermath of my good intentions were only part of my hurt. I asked myself, 'Why did it go wrong? I only wanted to be good!'

My mother always tried to stop my father hitting me and, though she also disciplined us, it was less traumatic.

When I was born, my father wanted to name me after a cricketer, while my mother wanted me named after a famous world statesman of the time. My mother apparently gave in to my father's wish, but unknown to him she registered me officially with her choice. While at home, I was called by his choice. My official name was not known to me until I started school.

My mother thought education for her children was of first importance. It was also through us that she could fulfil her educational ambitions, albeit indirectly. We were sent to our first school. It was in our local church. We used slates and recited our ABC. We saw pictures and read about 'Percy the Chick'. I liked reading, and the teacher gave me some of her books, which added another dimension to my so-far limited horizon. Whenever my mother went to market I had to miss school for the whole day. I cried every time until she allowed me to go every day.

My grandmother always made me read the Bible and the newspaper to her because her eyes were bad. Every evening it was a different chapter. I learned to read and spell very well. She always

7

sat in front of her kitchen, serene and meditative. A look of such calm, such righteousness. She could make us tremble with tales and folklore, tales of magic and murder, of demons and duppies or roaring-calves that tramped the lanes in the dead of night, searching for errant, little boys.

On Sundays we went to church. We put our best clothes on and invariably our faces would be lightly dusted with talc to stop perspiration. Church was also a social occasion, not least of all to us children, who had pocket-money for a snowball, a concoction of ice and syrup.

I started at a new school in the nearest town; though I was excited at this, my parents at this time went to England. It was then necessary for me to live with a family near school. I could not come to terms with my new guardians nor their lifestyle. Meals were an exercise in order and etiquette, as opposed to just satisfying a need. I could not wander outside, so I ran away to my grandmother. There I could be unrestricted in my wanderings: to climb the highest tree for a hitherto unreachable fruit; to eat a dozen of Mr Grant's oranges when there were thousands of my grandmother's within easier reach; to feel the wonder, the power, the fear of the unknown; danger and discovery.

Winston Robinson

■ Silver jet ■

I forget what month it was, August perhaps. I was five or six. The sun was always brighter when I was young. It hung in the sky like a huge, copper gong, making the road tar bubble up like small volcanoes. If you were careful you could gather up great lumps of it on a lollipop stick and throw it at the garage wall; if not, you got a good wallop off your old man for coming home all gummed up with the black stuff, not to mention the pain of having it scrubbed off.

Another favourite occupation of mine was prizing lumps of tarmac off the road, which came up in fist-sized lumps like black and grey peanut brittle. It didn't seem wrong to me, this casual vandalism, that is until I looked at the job overall: my God, had I done all that? There was a bald patch of about twenty feet square with the cobbles gleaming dully in the sun like grey-brown skull tops waiting to be dug up . . . or buried.

It was lovely that summer: hordes of breathless, excited kids running races round the block, jumping, fighting round the Lowry terraced streets; and the old men sat on the doorsteps with pints of tea and the evening news, sat on multicoloured cushions, florid, friendly, smiling. Timing races, taking part without actually running. The kids and the street went on for ever. It was a really lovely summer.

It happened that on this particular day I was as usual picking and pulling at the pebble-dashed tarmac, lost in my own little world, when the whole world seemed to tremble with a furious roaring. I was absolutely terrified at first, the sound was so vast and savage. But other kids joined me and we gathered enough courage to look for the sound's source and we raced around in circles as the sound faded away. As we walked despondently back to our own street, I asked an old man seated on his doorstep what the noise was. His face nearly fell in half when he smiled. 'It was a silver jet, son,' he said. An awed hush fell among us, and I could just see in my imagination how it clove its way through the blue sky. Emotions raced through me like a dozen fast horses and my heart pounded like a hammer. It must have shown plainly as I stood there transfixed, for the old man was watching my face, smiling.

After that 'Imagination Airways' jet I saw, seeing real ones was an anticlimax. Their shapes were never as good, nor could they fly as fast. Still I'll always be grateful to that old man for stoking up my daydream, for what he said, and still more for the way it was spoken.

Sammy Tierney

■ Losing a friend ■

It was about half-past three on a Tuesday afternoon. I was standing on the ground floor waiting for the lift. I was going up to the library on the eighth floor as it was my free period. Suddenly, I felt a hand pat me on the back of my shoulder. I turned around and saw it was David Mason, a good friend of mine. We were both the same age, fourteen, but that's where the similarity between us stopped. He was black, religious, shy and impeccably neat. I wasn't any of these things. Sometimes I envied him. He would smile that kind of awkward smile that would make his face light up and eyes shine. He was smiling it then.

'Hello, David,' I said. 'What are you doing here?'

'Hello, Mike,' he said, 'I'm going up to the library, what about you?'

'Yeah, so am I,' I said.

After we had spoken there was a moment's silence. We were thinking of something to say. Suddenly, I remembered a conversation we had last week about religion so I said to him,

'You don't really believe the earth was built in seven days, do you?'

'Of course I do,' he said. 'In the beginning God created the earth, heaven and man.'

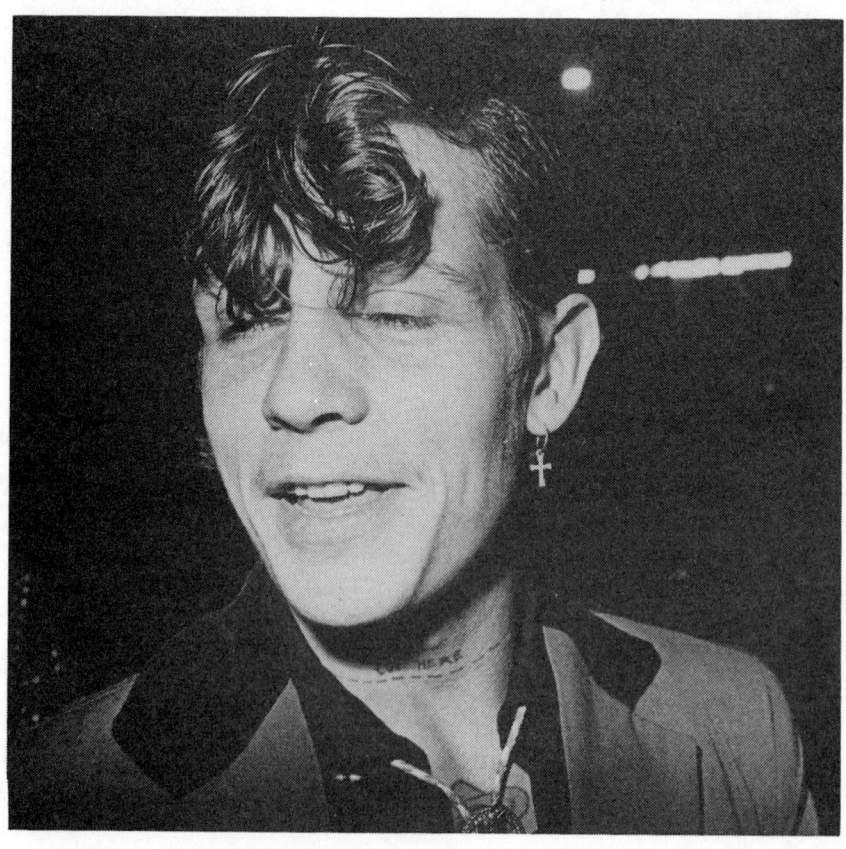

He began to launch into a long explanation of how we could tell God had made the earth. I was glad; that had been my intention – it would save having to make small talk, which bored me to tears. Anyway, I thought what he was saying was rubbish.

As he was explaining, I saw two youths coming towards us. One was black and the other was white. They both walked like they were tough, hands in pockets and heads turned arrogantly to the side. The moment I saw them I thought they were going to start trouble. They looked typical, self-image builders. There were many like them; I had met them over and over again. They all wanted to prove how tough they were to themselves, how big and brave they were to their friends and anyone else who was looking but hadn't noticed.

The white one wore a teddy-boy hairstyle, black drainpipe trousers, a brown leather jacket and heavy boots. His face was covered in spots. The black youth had a large afro, wore a white mac and black trousers with stripes. His face looked bitter. I wished they had gone some other way, I didn't want to get into any trouble. I looked at David to see if he had seen them. I don't think he had as he was so wrapped up in his explanation. They gradually came closer until they were almost next to us. Suddenly they stopped. My mouth went dry and I had a sick feeling in my stomach. I always felt like this when I sensed danger.

When they saw David wasn't taking notice of them, they didn't like it. They both walked over to him.

'You laughing at us?' the black one said.

David stopped talking, seeming to notice them for the first time.

'I was talking to him,' he answered.

'It looked to us like you were laughing,' the white one said, 'and we don't like people laughing at us.'

'Oh God,' I thought, 'they're looking for a fight.'

'I told you I was talking to him,' he said again.

I sensed fear in his voice.

'What you got in that bag?' the black one said, pointing to the briefcase David was carrying.

'Nothing,' said David.

'Well, if it's nothing let's see it,' said the white one.

I hoped they wouldn't turn their attention to me; I didn't want to get involved.

'No,' said David. 'Why should I?'

'Laughing and coming cheeky,' said the black one.

'Yeah,' said the white one. 'Cheeky little bastard.'

11

'I reckon he want trouble,' said the black one.

I looked at David. He was breathing heavily and I could almost hear his heart pounding. His eyes looked scared and he clutched the briefcase tightly to him.

'So let's give him . . .' started the white one.

Suddenly the black one jumped on David's back, while the white one began lashing into him with his boots. I knew I should help David, but couldn't, I was just too scared. I just ran. I was being a coward and knew it but couldn't help it. I ran out of the school gate and kept running. I ran until my chest burst and I could run no longer. I had run nearly halfway home.

When I had got my breath back I began to think. I thought of how cowardly I had acted. I was ashamed and disgusted with myself. How could I have done such a thing? How could I have left him like that? I had to admit to myself that I was cowardly and weak. I wondered how I was going to face him the next day. What could I say? What would he say to me? Would he ever speak to me? I thought these things as I walked home and thought about them all evening.

As usual tomorrow came too soon. I dreaded going to school that day – one of the few times I really had. I knew I was bound to see David Mason. We nearly always went out together at lunch. I saw him much sooner than I had expected. As I was going through the gate, so was he. I had that sick feeling in my stomach again. I noticed he had a slightly cut eye and a bruised cheek. He came up to me and began walking by my side. Suddenly I surprised myself and said, 'Look, David, about yesterday, I'm sorry there wasn't anything I could do.'

He was still smiling as usual. I felt like crying.

'I know,' he said. 'It doesn't matter. It was nothing.'

From the sound of his voice I knew that it did matter, and it was something. He was probably just being polite. I wish he hadn't been because I wanted him to blame me.

'Are you alright?' I asked.

'Yes,' he replied. 'I'm fine. Almost as soon as you went, a teacher came along, so I was lucky.'

'I'm glad,' I said. 'What about those two thugs?'

'They just ran away,' he replied. 'I'll probably never hear or see them again.'

'True,' I said.

After we had exchanged these words there was a silence. As we walked along I looked into his face. I could see that his smile was fixed and that behind it his face was sad. I thought he wasn't a good actor. Soon we had walked into school, and it was time for us to part. As he was leaving I said, 'Dinner as usual?'

'No,' he said. 'I've got to see someone. Sorry.'

As he left I knew he hadn't forgiven me. That very sentence condemned me. I thought that I had lost a good friend.

Philip Brackon

■ Glassworks ■

It was the best paid work in Knottingley. Everybody thought you'd best job in the world if you managed to get in glassworks but they didn't know what it was like. 'Chinese labour, Fred,' my mate used to say. I tell you retirement brought the happiest days of my life.

I started at fourteen in short trousers. I can remember running down Hill Top at 2.30 of a morning to start at 3.00 getting set pots ready for the 10 o'clock shift. We had our own potmakers. Mr Sidwell used to let you see him making the pots so far up but never how he put the crown on; he kept that a secret. His daughter would tread the clay for the pots with her bare feet.

Apprentice gatherers had to reach over and scoop out the last bit of metal at the bottom of the set pot. There'd be a gauze over the top, a flag we called it, to keep some of the heat off, but you'd still get wet and blistered on your chest. Apprentices had the dirty jobs to do like cooling the battery plungers in water; you needed rubber boots and apron for that. I'd be so tired when I went home, I couldn't lift my arms to wash myself.

It was the job of the apprentice to keep the men supplied with beer. I'd take eight tin cans on me fingers, pint or pint and a half, and go over to The Lamb. Jim Jagger would refill them at sixpence a pint. Once I dropped the lot. Jim said never mind and pulled me another set. I didn't know it, but he put the dropped ones on the slate as well, so I got a right telling off later. The men were always suspicious. 'This is a small pint, Taylor. Come here and let me smell at your breath!' The cans were used for tea as well as beer and no matter how you washed them out, they'd not be clean. Maillie, a big Geordie, was the biggest drinker and he had a filthy can; it always smelt of stewed tea. 'Come and fasten my boots, Taylor!' he'd shout at me. He was over twenty stone and couldn't reach so I'd have to do it. He'd a pair of great dirty legs on him, colour of ink. Only thing I hated more was lighting cigarettes for a man who'd lost half his face and an eye in the first world war. His cigarettes were always going out, and I'd have to relight the soggy things for him.

We'd all take bottles of tea to work. 'What shall I do wi' this bottle?' I asked on my first day.

'Put it agin furnace, lad. Keep it warm.'

It got that hot that when I came to take a drink out of it, it burnt a ring on my lips. After that I learned it was better to put it on side of the glory hole which was cooler. That wasn't perfect though; the tea tasted of oil from the glory-hole burners.

I fainted time and time again with the heat to start with. They had some habits to bring you round. One chap took me outside; I were going over, me eyes half-closed and I could just see he'd a mouthful of water he were going to blow all over me. Working close together, there was always the danger of getting the gathering iron caught up in your overalls. One time a gatherer was cleaning his iron in a bucket, turned round and splashed molten glass all up my legs. I never wore short trousers after that. You'd be sent to the lobby where they kept first aid but they knew no more about first aid than a ten year old. If you'd a blister on your hand as big as half a crown they'd just clip it off, worst thing you can do to a blister.

We were paid on piecework, negotiating a target with management beforehand. The boss would say, 'I want you to have a good try at this,' and we'd give it a go, not too fast. Once a target was fixed it couldn't be changed. Then we'd belt it away to get on bonus. The target for No. 3141, a five and a half inch dish, was 1500 in a shift, paid at three and ninepence halfpenny per hundred. On a good day we could make 2400 so we'd be on bonus, double the ordinary rate. The target was known as a 'doggie'. One shop would ask another, 'Have you got your doggie yet?'

The smaller the job the faster you had to work to get your money. Sometimes they'd go too fast at one end, and the shaper would have two pieces on his chair at the same time. One'd get cold and drop off and then the balloon'd go up as you'd all lost money. I'd send a message, 'Tell 'em they're working a bit too sharp.' Just to be awkward the gatherer would rest his iron and slow the pace completely until I had to say, 'Tell 'em they're too slow.' Then he could turn round and say, 'Mek up your mind. What do you want?'

We had a thirty ton oil-fired furnace which burned eighteen to twenty gallons of oil every hour. Every shop had a glory hole, a smaller firebox used to get a polish on the ware. You'd sweat that much you could get hold of your shirt off a washing line and it'd stand up on its own with salt in it. Fred Miller, my gatherer, always had white veins of salt on his trouser legs. I'd say, 'Have you jumped into 'em this morning, Fred? You can't have pulled 'em on.' The lehr was forty yards long, a conveyor belt which started off at same temperature as furnace and gradually cooled to the other end. When you opened the lehr doors the blast of hot air could burn off your eyebrows and eyelashes. There were a lot of cats about. They used to walk in to the lehr as far as they could and then sleep down the cool end. One day a lad was putting a piece in the hot end when a cat flew out over his shoulder! It hadn't a hair on it, and we had to drown it.

The heat was worst during the war when we couldn't open the windows after dark because of the blackout. At first we used to finish work when the air-raid sirens went but they were going nearly every night and too much production was lost so we had to work through. In the morning we could see the red glow in the sky from the bombing over towards Hull or Sheffield. In the war Bagley's was mostly put on making cells for batteries for submarines, field telephones and railway signal boxes. All domestic work had to be declared. If you did frivolous things like a flower jug you wouldn't call it that; it'd be a celery holder so as to pass as a utensil for food. My wife worked at Bagley's too. She was put on making steel shell cases. We were always under the impression they were gas shells, though I don't think they were ever used.

The last seven years I worked in the Training School, teaching young apprentices. Do you know, I liked that better than my own trade? There were times as a shaper when I could hardly face going back to work after the dinner break. I remember the big fire of 1954. I was standing at home in the garden at Ferrybridge when the sirens sounded and I thought, 'I hope that's our place gone up.' It was terrible that fire; the products in the finished store all melted down again; molten glass poured down the stairs. Gypsies got in and took the pieces that were still whole, but it was very dangerous. The glass had lost its annealing properties in the heat and the pieces could explode at any time.

Even before the fire things used to walk from the factory. One woman used to take out a trinket set every week and sell it round the pubs. Others used to smuggle out fruit dishes in their bras, so I'm told!

I worked at Bagley's for fifty-one years. You had to be tough to last. We had miners come and go, couldn't stand the heat. The boss's favourite saying was, 'We don't keep green pastures for tired horses.'

I met an old workmate on the bus the other day. All he said was 'Would you go back?' I just answered, 'Would you?'

Fred Taylor

■ Sweetmaking ■

I probably would have been an office worker when I left school at fourteen if my best friend, Lizzie, hadn't landed herself a job at Bullock's. She told me how the girls all sat at long tables and discussed boys and make-up. 'And you can eat as many sweets as you like!' That did it; despite Mum's disapproval I went to Bullock's. All Dad said was, 'If they take on our Nellie they'll be bankrupt in a month. She'll eat all their profits.'

Bullock's was a huge place. I started in the boiling room five flights up. The stairs went round in squares; they went round a lift which kept going up and down but it seemed to be reserved for transporting goods. I was given a white cap and apron and took my place with a row of white robed girls rolling sugar sticks. They were a friendly lot but didn't seem interested in sampling the little bits which sometimes broke off and, being new, I didn't like to ask if I could eat them.

I soon learned how to weigh and pack the boiled sweets into glass jars. The better ones were wrapped separately in cellophane but the others were packed straight into jars. I'd only been there a few days when Elsie (she was in charge of the packing room) said, 'Take these sweets to Room 18.'

'Where's that?' I asked.

'Three flights down.'

'Where are the tops for the jars?'

16

'They'll have special ones put on downstairs. Now get you.'

I approached the swing doors and my arms being full I turned round and put my back to the door and pushed my way through. What I didn't realise in my ignorance was that it would swing back and catch me a thwack in the rear. I staggered, put out my hands to save myself going down the stairs and lost the jars. How the glass didn't break I'll never know but they did roll over, and all the sweets shot down the stairs. I collapsed on the top step in tears. I didn't know what to do. I thought I might have to go to prison. Tommy, one of the young lads, rescued me with a brush and a cardboard box. 'Get 'em swept up afore anybody comes.' Fear quickened my hands, and we soon got the sweets back in the jars. 'On your way,' said Tommy, 'you're lucky not to be caught.'

Bullock's was famous for making rock. The sugar was boiled in huge cauldrons with gas jets underneath, some pink and some white. It was poured on a metal table to cool a little, and then two men would stretch it and throw it between them. Every time they pulled it the texture changed and it became more soft and silky.

The women and girls worked at long, metal tables dusted with confectionery powder so the mixture wouldn't stick. A pink piece was put down the middle of the table, then cut-out, elongated letters in red interspersed with white, then a white core, making a cylinder of rock. It'd be about twenty-four inches in diameter to begin with. Then we'd start to roll. As it got longer more and more women would be rolling until there was a row of twenty working together. You'd start with one cylinder then as it got thinner another would be put to it until you were rolling twenty or thirty together. Everyone had to keep their sleeves rolled right up as you used the whole length of your arms, stretching right across the table. By the time you'd rolled it to an inch wide the letters were in the right place and a man with a two foot pair of shears cut it into lengths. The ends were snipped off while they were still warm and soft, but I didn't get the chance to eat them. They were sold off separately. We did rock for all over: Bridlington, Scarborough, Filey, Whitby, all the Yorkshire places of course; and Cleethorpes, Blackpool, Felixstowe and Aberystwyth, that was a squash to fit in.

And this eating business. I hadn't had time for more than a nibble so far. Liquorice Allsorts were always a favourite of mine so when I was moved to that department I was really keen. As we started going down to what seemed the bowels of the earth my enthusiasm waned. It was a huge room. Everything in it was huge. There were huge tables on which huge layers of black liquorice were interspersed with huge layers of coloured confections. These were passed through giant rollers and cutters. I was terrified by the size of everything. And it was so dark. There were no windows, only a few electric light bulbs strung at intervals on a wire.

Another girl, older and very unfriendly, instructed me in my duties. I think the gloom of the place had invaded her spirit as it had began to invade mine. I felt trapped, in with all those machines, in the dark and the noise. I used to go to the toilet, kneel up on the seat, open the window and lean out into the fresh air. I longed to go back and play in the fields and the park again.

Eventually I summoned up all my courage and went to tell the foreman I was going to leave. I was halted in my tracks by a large notice on the wall. It said that Bullock's was closing down. All employees were given a week's notice. Had Dad's prophecy come true?

Nellie Oldroyd

■ Satch ■

It was the autumn of 1959. You know, in this youth-work game, the people that you're catering for, the clients, tend to go off to the parks and run away like birds in the spring and summer. You don't tend to see them together in big heaps until the autumn comes. This particular night, the lads bought in a fella they called Satch. He was a tall guy; he was a bit older than the normal recruit that we had in this club. He was a fella of about twenty-one, twenty-two, and he was dressed in a rather old-fashioned way. He'd always got an earplug stuck in his ear and a lead running off it, as though he was always listening to music and he wasn't really with us. He always carried his head slightly on one side, very gentlemanly, and rather old-fashioned. I didn't know how the lads had collected him because he seemed quite out of character.

He asked me if he could join the club so I said, 'Yes.' I said,

'You're a little bit old for our lot.'

He said, 'That's alright, I'd like to come.'

He didn't do very much. He arrived and was usually fairly helpful. Then one day I was packing up. It was getting on for half-past ten at night, and I'd got to carry a lot of junk across to my office in another part of the campus of the school.

He said, 'Can I help you, Skip?'

I said, 'Yes, you can, sure.'

He got hold of a crate of coke or empties or something and walked after me across the campus area. On the way, I began to have the feeling that he'd got some reason to be coming with me that wasn't really connected with what I was doing, which was really packing up. As I got closer to the west wing of the school, I had to open a section of the school with a master-key and climb some stairs. He was right up behind me, and I had this foreboding that there was something in the air that was a bit unusual. When I got into my office to write down some figures, the attendance, how much money had been paid in subscriptions and all this stuff on my night-sheet, I didn't take my eyes off him. I made sure he was in front of me, but it was a bit difficult, you know, when you want to concentrate on writing. I turned to him suddenly, and he had his hand inside his jacket. I knew about this sort of thing from my days in the army. The Arabs used to carry a hand down there and on the end of that hand was usually a knife. I thought to myself, 'Surely Satch hasn't got a knife?' Anyway, I got up and got away, nothing happened to me. I saw him to the door, I locked the gate up, caught the bus, and off he went.

The thought that he was a bit of a strange character stayed with me. Then later he began to 'fantasize', to tell me all sorts of strange stories about what he'd done. He'd conducted the National Youth Orchestra. He brought me a record, and showed me a caption which he'd obviously dubbed onto this record: 'This is conducted by . . .'. I won't tell you his name. I took all this in my stride because when you've got three to four hundred members, you always get two or three percent who are a little bit strange. Anyway, I'm strange so there's a bit of common ground there.

At that time, I was running a fairly successful rock-session on a Thursday night. Satch used to like to come because he would usually meet up with the young lads, the Teds who'd picked him up in the park and brought him in. On this particular Thursday, my girlfriend of the time was taking the money on the door. I moved over later in the evening to ask how things were going, and she said, 'I've lent a book to Satch. He wanted to read about architecture, and I've lent him a book.' This sort of gave me a bizarre picture of the young man. It was quite unusual. I'd hear on the grapevine that he was a lift-operator in a great factory and that he was quite a loner. Nobody got anywhere near him.

That following week, on the Tuesday night, I had to go away from the club. I always liked to be there when the action was on at night, and they wanted me to be present, so I made arrangements for the boys to cover the job. I got one or two helpers and I went away merrily to my basketball meeting.

At the end of the meeting, somewhere around half-past nine, a fella said,

'Do you want a lift back?'

I was usually the last to leave the school so I said,

'I'll go back, just to see the school's alright'. And I went back. When I got to my hall where I did my main work, the hall called the South Hall, there was a quiet about the place which was unusual. I went to one of the helpers and said,

'What's the matter?'

He said, 'The police have been in and taken away Satch.'

So I said, 'What happened?'

He said, 'We were playing darts with big Lenny over there, and this big fella came in. Everyone could see it was a copper. He said, "Is your name . . .?" and Satch said, "Yes." So he said, "Would you like to come with me?" '

'What happened then?' I said.

'Well, he turned to one of the fellows and said, "Take my shot, I'll be back in a minute." And he didn't come back.'

Well, this worried me. I wondered what it was all about and I was on Satch's side anyway. The following morning, I'm buzzing around Parliament Street, and who should be on point duty but one of my ex's, Brian . . . in his uniform and all his bits and pieces. I walked across into the middle of the road and I said,

'Brian, they took away one of my lads last night.'

He said, 'Is his name . . .?'

I said, 'Yes.'

He left the point where he was controlling the traffic, came over to the pavement, and said, 'You know what they've got him for, don't you?'

I said, 'No.'

'You know that shopkeeper on Bentinck Road they found fastened to the counter with a knife – they got him for that.'

Gordon Clay

20

■ Day of the carnival ■

I was sitting down staring into two worlds. The real world of ITV sport and horse racing and my own imaginative world of what would be going on at the Notting Hill carnival, imagining dancing in the streets and music in my ears. Suddenly I pulled myself out of my imaginary world and decided to get ready to go to the carnival.

Whilst journeying through the city, I was reflecting back on a past conversation I had had with some friends and how I remembered that one of them had said that they thought that a fight might break out at the carnival. This thought lingered at the back of my mind.

I had decided that if any of my friends were there, then they would most likely be down by the flyover arches because under the arches there were groups playing music and food being sold. I knew this from last year.

I proceeded down Ladbroke Grove towards Portobello Road where the flyover arches were. The first thing I noticed was that there weren't half as many people as last year when the streets were rammed and not much traffic was running down Ladbroke Grove because it was difficult to get through. My reasoning for this was last year's lack of organisation when many people got squeezed and squashed in the half million crowd.

Because of the smaller amount of people and last year's lesson, this carnival appeared much more organised. People were lined along the pavement and the roads were kept clear. But another thing that struck my mind as I was walking down Ladbroke Grove past crowds of happy colourful people was the obvious presence of large amounts of policemen ('Bull' as we call them, we being black youths) and I was sure that such large numbers of bulls weren't necessary. There were more bulls this year than last and yet there were much fewer people. The bulls must have been anticipating another large crowd. As I neared the flyover arches, I could hear music, bass mostly, coming from under the flyover and I could see big crowds of people in the area, dancing, eating and just standing up listening to the music.

I wandered round the arches listening to the different sounds and noticed that this area attracted a lot of youths who'd also come to listen to the music. But it also attracted pickpockets and muggers; they were recognizable because of the fact that they travelled in gangs of about twenty and possessed weapons which could be seen bulging in their back pockets or, in some cases, were partly visible.

I did, in fact, see a mugging which made me feel very bad inside. A gang of youths surrounded a middle-aged white man and hustled him through the gang, going through his pockets at the same time. The reason it made me feel bad inside was because it spoiled the fun of the carnival for a lot of people who had come to enjoy themselves.

I decided to wait with the crowd for the procession to pass. It wasn't long before I heard the sound of calypso music and happy voices. I nudged my way through the large crowd to get a closer look. In the front of the procession were dancing people dressed in beautiful brightly-coloured uniforms, waving standards. Some people wore tribal costumes of straw skirts and were carrying spears. Some were dressed in white feathered costumes imitating birds, and others were in beautiful lace costumes with large wings imitating butterflies. There were many different kinds of costumes and standards. Behind the brightly costumed people was a large steel band playing very rhythmic music which made me feel very excited and happy.

The calypso music and the sight of all the people enjoying themselves was too much for me. This was my scene and I had to join in. I stepped into the road and soon became one of the happy, dancing people I was watching not long before. It was brilliant, I'd never enjoyed myself so much for a long time. I didn't see many of my friends whilst following the procession, but it didn't matter; I met many people and made a lot of friends. The only thing that chilled the atmosphere of the carnival air was the sight of so many bulls scattered all over the area. It made me feel restricted as though I was being watched closely. It also made me feel as though a lot of crime went on in the area which wasn't true; everyone was just enjoying themselves, dancing and singing. There was no crime in evidence to me, not there anyway.

I was enjoying myself so much that I didn't realise time had gone so fast and in the distance I could see successive changes in the night sky. I knew that night would soon be on me and I began to wonder where I could catch a bus to go home. But I didn't want to go home, I wanted to stay longer and enjoy myself more. I decided to stay on a little longer which I knew would mean being late. Night soon came and I was still enjoying myself with some of my new-found friends. An old man came up the street and started shouting things about how there'd been a fight down the road between police and youths. Most people, including myself, didn't really take this seriously and just carried on the festivities. But as I neared the scene where the bright blue and yellow lights were flashing, this excited me greatly and I began to wonder whether there really was a fight between police and youths. I decided to run ahead of the procession to see what was going on. As I came to the corner of the road, a large crowd of girls came down singing 'Police and Thieves' (a reggae song about police and thieves fighting in the streets). Now I was sure there had been a fight. I ran faster up the road and noticed that scattered all over the streets were tiny crystals of glass and shattered fragments of brick. I also noticed that many shop windows were smashed and in the distance I could see a car burning wildly and as I neared it, I could see firemen trying to put the fire out.

There weren't many people in this part of the street. But I could hear shouting coming from the arches area. I ran to the arches to see what was going on and saw a very large crowd of people all standing and staring up the road. I heard a roaring sound; people began shouting 'Bulls coming, bulls coming' and turned towards and passed me. I watched the faces of people as they passed. Some young girls and women looked terrified, their mouths gaped wide open and their eyes glaring. Many were screaming as though they were being tortured.

The men were running and looking back at the same time. Some of them had frightened faces but mostly they looked puzzled as though stuck in a maze. When the wave of people had gone past me, I saw a large crowd of police in the distance ducking and running frantically in different directions like blind men. They were running from a hail of bricks and bottles being thrown by youths on building sites and the flyover. Some police began throwing bricks back at the youths. I noticed a young lad sitting on the fence watching the violent scene and seeing him get toppled off the fence by a brick. I don't know whether the brick that knocked him off was thrown by a policeman or one of the youths. But I felt very sorry for the kid and sickened by the scene. I don't know what happened to the child who got knocked off the fence because immediately after I had to run – the battlefield was encroaching upon me. I ran down an alleyway leading into Ladbroke Grove and near the tube station so I could get a train home.

To my surprise, this part of the street was empty with the exception of a few police closing down the station and seemingly waiting for something. Suddenly, like an army assault, coach and car loads of police began coverging on the area. They stepped out and formed into small groups. The policemen who came out of the coaches had long, leather sheaths hanging down their sides and from these they withdrew long, light-coloured truncheons. I was very frightened by now and I thought I was going to get picked up by the police on 'Sus.' There was no way I was going to get out of this area without having to walk through a group of policemen. I was standing by a wall, thinking of what to say when the police picked me up, what my mother would think if I got nicked and whether I'd get beaten up down Police Central.

A large policeman noticed me and came up tapping his truncheon in the palm of his hand, shouting, 'Get out, go on get out!' I ran a small way up the road and came to another small crowd of policemen. I walked past them, thinking I'd get nicked, but to my surprise, I didn't. I reached a bus stop and waited with about eight other people for a bus. We'd been waiting for about an hour, wondering whether the buses were running, when a policeman came and told us that the bus service had been stopped due to the debris in the streets and the risk of violence breaking out along the bus route. The time was now about 10.30 p.m. and I didn't know where I could catch a bus to go home. I'd asked around but nobody knew. Someone told me my best bet was to catch a taxi but I didn't have enough money for the fare. Just when I'd given up home and was anticipating walking to the West End (which was about two miles away), I saw a friend of mine, Neville. Neville said that if I stuck with him I could get a lift home from his friend who was somewhere around. I stuck with Neville and we came across a band with a lot of followers dancing merrily. We mingled in with the followers and were soon dancing and enjoying ourselves. In the crowd of followers I found many of my friends and Neville found his friend, Denver, who was to give us a lift home. We followed the band until it finished playing at about 12.30 a.m. and then I got a lift home.

Lennox Miller

■ When you don't feel like a foreigner ■

It is never easy being a foreigner in a country; it is even more difficult when you don't feel like a foreigner.

I am an Asian girl, originally from India, though I was born here in England eighteen years ago. I live in relative comfort in an exceptionally nice area of the town with all the amenities and many of the luxuries at my disposal. I enjoy my life here and would find it difficult to imagine living in another country.

I think people in all spheres of life are bound to experience prejudice at one time or another, be it for their race, colour or creed but perhaps we Asians are subject to prejudice in all these areas. I have found that there are two main types of prejudice: the kind that is expressed in loud, explicit and often violent tones, the other a more subtle though no less expressive type. The former I do not experience directly very often and as yet never in its violent form. It is intimidating to have to walk past a group of young 'skinheads' and suffer being called names such as 'smelly paki' or 'chocolate drop' or have to cross the road to avoid a group of older 'skinheads'. I believe these human beings who look and sound as they do are as much a pest to English people as they are to us.

The second form of prejudice is the type I encounter from my good friends. My best friends are all English and white and when they use phrases like, 'I don't think of you as being an Indian, I mean you don't smell of curry or speak with an Indian accent', they often astonish me in their naivety at thinking that all Indians are like that. Another interesting example of prejudice amongst friends is a conversation I had with a boy I was going out with at the time. He simply adored me and I him, but he could not accept my being superior to him in any way. We were discussing our 'O' level results and although he did not do as well as me he insisted that had he worked harder or even worked at all he would have done better than me. I thought at first that this was because I was a girl, but from later conversations I realised that it was because I was an Indian girl.

Parental care, to all appearances, is much more protective and thus restrictive in Indian homes than in English ones. From my own experience I find it extremely annoying, especially since my friends are not treated in the same way. My parents insist on knowing where I am when I go out, though not necessarily who I am with, what time I will be home and how I am getting home. Whereas my friends are allowed to walk home after a party, although they must tell their parents at what time they will be home. Personally, I find this an overprotective part of my parents' nature, but of course, having spoken to many other Indian girls in my college, this constitutes complete freedom in comparison with them. Naturally, since most of us are influenced to a high degree by the views of our parents, maybe many of my own ideas are simply extensions of those of my parents and often my own ideas are in conflict with those of my friends.

Marriage of course is a major topic of conversation for girls of my age, since within the next few years we all hope to be married. My friends find my marriage arrangements interesting because they are never sure whether or not a marriage is to be arranged for me. My views on this subject have changed over the years. Until a few years ago I felt arranged marriages to be very unromantic and I couldn't understand how couples could be content with this arrangement. I then began speaking to girls who considered an arranged marriage to be acceptable, in some cases even desirable. Having increased in years and experience, my views have been somewhat tempered. I now believe that, from reading recent statistics, 'love' marriages are not more successful than arranged marriages; however, I feel that it is the freedom of choice in a 'love' marriage that makes me covet one. I feel that I should have a complete choice in the man with whom I am to spend the rest of my life, the chance to make up my own mind about the person I could be happy with, the freedom to decide my future, be it the right or the wrong choice.

Rita

Capturing the moment

There are five pieces in this section. Each deals with a brief experience which the authors have tried to capture in words. The experiences described provoke various emotional responses in the writers: exhilaration, defeat, sadness or resignation. In their use of language the writers attempt to go beyond the truthful and accurate record aimed at by the authors of the pieces in 'Keeping a personal record'. They not only experiment with language, and with the meanings of words, but they express their feelings more openly. The writing is personal and subjective, although the approach is still 'realistic' and 'true to life'.

■ Moment ■

He leaned back from his work to check it and as he did a pair of swifts spun a confused flight path in the clear blue. He watched them for a moment amazed that they didn't crash into one another. Standing completely upright, his eyes spanned the horizon. Ugly as it was, it was a view that, if the scaffold had not taken him there, he wouldn't have seen, and besides, Nature encroached here and there on the city's environs, leaving a bending tree here, a patch of grass there and the feel of the crisp wind everywhere.

The wind was cold on the skin but not sharp and did not pierce his jacket. It reminded him of the sea and he enjoyed its freshness, its cleanness and standing on the scaffold high above the ground, he mused on being a sea captain full of adventure, travelling expanses of ocean, to strange green belted shores.

The world somehow seemed better today, it felt new and clear, robbed of its pain and suffering, its hate and fear, its corrupt and power-mad masters. Today it was raw like a baby, fresh born, ready to be grappled and shaped by a new breed, a new ideology and a new spirit. It stood as a challenge to those, like him, who would mould it with care, build it with sense, develop it with reason and balance all with love. 'Ay, today was a day of hope', he thought, 'a day to renew one's faith in a better life, a better way, a day to say to all other days, we don't want you as you are, we want you different.'

He looked down at his work, for that too, with the wind, the view and all, had inspired him to these thoughts. He was aware of his craft today, he wasn't a machine laying bricks, he wasn't a nobody, just a soppy old bricklayer, a mere tradesman – he was part artist, part artisan. He had worked in a quick happy rhythm, absorbed, aware of everything so that his tools were like a painter's brush, a part of him, held with grace and care, used with love and precision. He eyed his work knowing that, if he placed his level down, the bubble would sit perfectly in the middle as it touched each brick square on. He stepped back and admired the cross joints, even and equal, course after course, as if drawn, the other almost perfect in line. The even bricks glowed their redness in the early morning sun and gave off a warmth and richness, locked in their black, smooth joints.

'Neat bit of work', he thought to himself, and a feeling of pride swam over him. 'This job is worth it for moments like these,' he whispered to himself, 'when you feel a part of your work and a part of the world, an important part of the world – a world in which if it were run on a different basis, moments like these would be more frequent.'

He gazed at the clocktower. 'It'll soon be teatime,' he thought and that satisfied him for it's nice to have a hot cup of tea and a chat with some of the lads. A minute had passed since he saw the swifts.

He spun the leather handled trowel in his hand, as was his habit, looked down at his work, bent down to the mountain of black mortar on the board, flicked the required amount to the middle of the trowel, picked up a brick and automatically on the way up, buttered the brick and laid it neatly and lightly on the waiting bed and line, scraped off the excess and stretched for another brick.

John Keane

■ Cruelty on a summer's day ■

It was a lovely day in summer, hazy with sunshine, warm, peaceful and still. Not even a leaf moved on the trees, and no discordant sound of civilization could be heard. Enjoying my walk in the countryside, I decided to take a rest, sat down on the warm sweet smelling grass in a meadow off the beaten track and looked around.

Such peace was unbelievable. I let myself observe and enjoy the beauty all around me: the faint scent of honeysuckle and bluebells; the hum of the bees as they moved from one wild flower to another; butterflies in all their beauty, flying about idly in the sunshine and small insect life working away industriously on the ground.

There was a stir in the grass not far from me, a flutter of wings and into the air a bird flew high up into the sky. I followed its flight with some difficulty through the hazy sunshine, then it seemed to stand still and burst into song.

There was only one bird who could do that, a lark. Its lilting melody spread over the countryside. On and on it sang, a tiny little mite, with a gift no other bird could emulate. He was no actor seeking an audience or applause, only for him the pleasure of serenading his loved one nesting in the tall grass many miles below.

In the warm stillness of this summer's day, in what seemed to me to be a small corner of heaven, it could hardly be supposed that anything would shatter such peace and harmony, and I lay back and closed my eyes. Suddenly a discordant note awoke me: the sound of human voices. I sat up just in time to see two men with guns under their arms appear as they jumped over a boundary wall. They began walking slowly across the meadow. On they came, indifferent to the beauty all around them as they trampled over the meadow, crushing the sweet flowers beneath their feet, intent only on killing. They stopped, then peered high up into the heavens, searching through the haze for the tiny little mite that acted as a challenge to their egos. The beauty of the song held no interest for them, only a cruel desire to put an end to its melody.

Suddenly there was an ominous silence. The lark stopped singing. Evil seemed to permeate the air. In the hush that followed there was an expectancy that sacrilege was about to be committed in this small garden of heaven.

Swift as an arrow, the lark came out of the sky, straight down at the men. It fluttered its wings, then flew back up again. Taken by surprise, they failed to bring their guns into action, but as the bird flew down at them again, one man got the bird in his sights, and fired.

There was a thunderous sound of gunshot, which echoed over the valley. Pellets seared the air, and the small heavenly songster bravely flew on, faltered and fell to the ground.

'Got him,' shouted one, jubilantly, as they both raced away from the path they were originally going to take in their eagerness to search for their victim.

Kicking the tall grass aside in their vain search, they gave up the effort, and turned off in the direction of a wood, on the other side of the meadow.

I got up and ran towards the spot where the bird had fallen, hoping against hope that the bird might not be too badly wounded. It took me a little while to find it, but when I did, I could see what little strength it had left. It had curled itself up into a tiny little ball in a very thick clump of grass. As I picked it up gently, its warm, little, brown body lay helpless in my hand. I felt utterly sad and insignificant compared to this songster that would never grace the heavens again, and when its little head sagged over my hand, I realized nothing could be done.

When I had finished burying it, I looked over to where I had been. Somewhere over there was a nest with another lark looking after its young. Was it, I wondered, possible that the mother had accepted the fact that the father had given his life by luring the men away from the path they were about to take towards her nest and, in so doing, saved them?

Frank Hayes

■ The rest is history ■

There is a jug and there is milk in it and there is cream on the top and a fly floats in it. It is a hot day and the jug is on a wooden kitchen table. The room is dark and cool. The house is in the country.

A woman in a paisley apron, about fifty, plump and cosy with greying hair in a bun, is gazing in dismay at the fly in the milk and decides it must be thrown away; then she decides to get the fly out and keep the milk to put in her bath, like Cleopatra bathing in asses' milk.

The kitchen has stone flags on the floor.

The woman rolls up her sleeves; she is wearing a white, cotton blouse and begins to flour a board on the table. She punches and pummels a lump of light yellow dough. Then she takes a rolling pin, which is wooden and has two red handles, from the table drawer, clattering the knives and forks inside as she does so. She sprinkles flour on the rolling pin, and humming, 'I'll be seeing you', she begins to roll the pastry. First it stays in a fat lump, then gradually it gets flatter and thinner. As she goes along, she sprinkles on more flour; the pastry must not stick to the rolling pin. Her paisley apron gets all floury. She pushes a stray hair out of her eyes and leaves a streak of flour on her forehead. She delicately lifts a thin slice of the pastry and flops it down into a pyrex dish, greased to opacity. Then she goes to the draining board where there are two Bramley apples and a lemon.

She rummages through the drawer and finds the special knife, stabs it through the first apple and deftly removes the core. She slowly winds her way round the apple, making a long, green snake of peel. Then she does the same to the other one. She begins to sing softly, 'You made me love you, I didn't wanna do it, I

33

didn't wanna do it', and reaches in the drawer for a sharp knife. She is smiling and 'la-la-la-ing' because she has forgotten the words. She cuts the apples in slices and lays them on the pastry, then she cuts the lemon in half and squeezes it over the apples. She sprinkles more flour on the remaining pastry and rolls it out, then pulls a sheet of it, like a membrane, from the board. She places it squarely on top of the apples, then, like a waiter with a tray of drinks, she balances the dish on the fingertips of her left hand, up in the air, while she cuts off the overhanging pastry with the sharp knife in the other hand. One twirl and it is done. She rifles through the drawer again to find a brush and a fork. She cracks the egg on the side of a glass bowl and it slithers in. She beats it with the fork, making a tinny, irritating noise, brushes the top of the pastry with it and makes some small cuts in the crust.

She has remembered to put the oven on so that it will be hot. On opening the door she sees the quivering blue flames. The pie goes into the oven and she sets about clearing up the kitchen.

It is a sunny day. She notices this when she empties the rubbish in the dustbin outside the back door. The dog is lying asleep by the wall. A plane flies overhead through a pale blue sky.

She turns and goes back into the kitchen, leaving the back door open. She goes through it to the other room, which is cooler, and turns on the radio.

It's about quarter-past eleven.

A man's voice says: 'You can imagine what a bitter blow it is to me that all my long struggle to win peace has failed. Yet I cannot believe there is anything more, or anything different that I could have done, that would have been more successful.'

She goes to the window, his voice droning on in the background: 'For it is evil things that we shall be fighting against, brute force, bad faith, injustice, oppression and persecution. And against them I am certain that right will prevail.'

She clicks off the radio and goes to check the pie.

Sue May

■ Helen ■

I first met Helen one cold, damp, November afternoon, walking up the hill towards the library. She was muffled in a large, heavy, tweed coat, and long scarf half-covering her face. As we drew level, she pulled down the scarf, scraping her mouth, and the scarlet lipstick smudged onto her chin.

Her voice, low and husky asked, 'Can you spare 10p for a cuppa?'

Our eyes met: hers grey and indifferent; mine, I suspect, blank and wide.

'I'm sorry,' I replied, jolting back after thinking how on earth I was going to make the dentist's, cook dinner and get to the Friends Centre all in one and a half hours. I had taken far too long choosing my books.

'Got 10p for a cuppa, please?'

I felt in my pocket and only finding a few coppers, I opened my purse. As I handed her 50p, I thought to myself, 'I've never seen a tramp wearing lipstick before.' She almost snatched the coin and, pulling the scarf back over her mouth, walked up the hill.

It was several weeks before I was to meet her again, and a New Year. January 5th had been a very cold day, but the air was crisp and dry as I walked home through the park. There she was, the tramp woman, sitting on the concrete ground gazing into the half-frozen pond.

'Hello,' I said, slowly passing her. 'How are you?' I realised at once what a stupid thing I'd said as she very obviously wasn't alright. Her face was purple and swollen, her hands were blue and her feet were bound in filthy rags. Her eyes blinked. I stopped and turned towards her. I could see she remembered me: she half raised her arm and waved her hand, which I mistook at first as a gesture, the 'clear off and leave me alone' kind.

I stood awkward, feeling foolish almost. Then seeing the grey eyes brim then gush with tears, she raised her arm again and I realised she was asking me to help her up. I tried in vain, first by standing at her back and putting my hand under her arm pits, but she was so laden down with clothes it was impossible. Then I held out my hands to her – her grip was too weak – I knew she was very ill.

I bent down and said, 'I'm going to get some help. What is your name?'

Her voice came weak and childlike, 'Helen, my name is Helen.'

I ran to the phone box on the edge of the park. My fingers, cold and stiff, dialled three nines. I ran back down to the park to Helen who was now no longer sitting but lying in a crumpled heap like a pile of old clothes. I knelt down.

'Helen, Helen,' I called gently, 'someone is coming to help you. You'll soon be tucked up nice and warm.'

I felt guilty not knowing how else to comfort her. Her eyes closed, and the tears she shed made thin, white streaks down her grey, dirty face. I called 'Helen,' again. She raised her hand and her fingers touched my cheek.

Help came in the shape of two young policemen, then the ambulance crew.

'Drunk?' They directed the question to the policemen, but my reply came quickly back,

'No, she's ill,' and my voice almost whispered the next words, 'and I think she's in pain.'

'Not any more, love,' the man with the small, dark bag said. 'She's dead.'

Margaret Bearfield

■ Jack at the Palace ■

Jack humped his suitcase off the shuddering bus and paused to tighten his overcoat against the slanting rain. After turning down a glistening side street, past a huddle of back to backs, he soon found himself in Newtown Row.

Adolf Hitler had spared the Palace during his slum demolition campaign of 1941, but the Luftwaffe was the last thing Jack had on his mind. Tonight he'd soon be in action against a more hostile enemy, a live audience.

He smiled grimly as he caught sight of his name in bold type on the poster in the foyer. He was billed to do a twenty minute comedy spot immediately after the main feature film. Not that Jack reckoned much on Cine Variety. Few cinemas had dressing-rooms, and trying to change your trousers balanced on one leg in the darkened wings was often perilous. But then, Jack reckoned, four quid was four quid even if you did end up doing your act with your trousers on back to front.

Arthur the doorman jerked his head towards the paybox. 'The tickets 've bin sellin' like burnt cakes, Jack,' he muttered. 'And they'm only in tonight 'cos it's chuckin' it down outside. Mind yo, Jack, it's bin like it all wik. Now last wik we 'ad 'em queuin' out into the 'oss road. Not this wik, though. It's a right duff film, it is.'

Jack nodded knowingly. He'd heard it all before.

'One thing, though, Jack,' he continued. 'They'm mostly soldiers in tonight. Territorials. Reckon they'll want a bit of . . . you know what I mean, Jack?'

Jack knew what he meant. He'd heard it all before.

As the last few frames of the main film clattered through the projector, Jack moistened his lips slowly. There would be no introduction, no stuttering piano and drum roll to accompany his entrance, just a solitary spot lighting the curtain and out front, a seething silence.

Jack breathed deeply, and was on.

The audience – all fourteen of them – sat unmoved. The silent minority.

'Did I ever tell you about me mate, Charlie . . .?'

Nothing. A seat creaked.

'Is there anyone out there . . .?'

Nothing again. The silence was relentless.

Punch line followed punch line.

'Come on now . . . I can hear you breathin'.'

Jack laughed. But he laughed alone. Two rows back a thick-eared sergeant flicked a soggy Woodbine at the stage.

'Tek 'im orf. We doe want to listen to all that. Give us a bit o' rough stuff.'

'Yeah,' another rasping voice. 'Give us a bit o' blue stuff.'

But Jack hardly heard them. They were only going to get what he wanted to give them. And it wasn't the rough stuff.

Gag after gag vanished like cigar smoke, but he didn't falter. Finally he ended with a couple of belters and shuffled off to a sitting ovation from a cleaner in the back stalls, and a derisive groan from everywhere else.

Arthur was waiting. 'Yo died a death out there tonight, Jack.'

Jack nodded. 'Well, if they want the rough stuff, Arthur, they should tek themselves down to the Aston Hipp. If they just want some nerker to shovel 'oss muck at 'em they should goo to the stable. It's the same thing. But they won't gerrit from me. Even if I do die the death.'

Arthur unlocked the stage door to let Jack and his case through. 'Yo'm right there, Jack. But don't forget, though. Yo died a death all right . . . but at least yo died with dignity.'

Jack smiled and walked into the night.

Chris Flanagan
(Jack Bates, the Brummagem dialect comedian, is now in his seventies and living in retirement in Handsworth.)

Telling a story

There are fifteen stories in this section. Most of the stories use realistic, everyday experience as their starting-point, e.g. home and family situations (' "D for Dad" ' and 'Letting go'), a school setting (' "For those in peril" ' and 'The confirmation class') and contact with the wider community ('A visitor', 'Death came to dinner' and 'Thank Gawd for the National Health').

A number of the stories are set at work: in a building site ('A man like Mulloy'); a newspaper office ('A change of heart'); a factory ('Nothing surprised me at Grumpton's') and a colliery ('The water rats'). Each of the four authors uses the workplace as a springboard to go off in different narrative directions. 'A man like Mulloy' relates the story of a man working in a 'foreign' country who finds out where his heart and values really lie. 'A change of heart' traces gradual disillusionment with a particular type of high-pressure selling; then in two of the stories, 'Nothing surprised me at Grumpton's' and 'The water rats', the conflict is direct and uncompromising.

In the last three stories of the section, the authors have used their imaginations either to recreate a society that has vanished ('Victorian piece') or to tell an unusual story about the present ('Jimmy takes the lead' and 'The human factor').

These fifteen stories represent widely varying approaches to the craft of story-telling. Some aim for a simple and direct 'slice-of-life' approach where the story more or less speaks for itself; the impact of these pieces depends on the accurate and authentic observation of people in particular surroundings. Others are more consciously shaped to produce particular effects; the writers reflect on the stories they tell and implicitly invite the reader to share their attitudes. The latter approach is neither better nor more sophisticated than the first one; it is just different. These are points worth considering not only while you are reading these stories, but when you start writing narrative pieces of your own.

■ 'For those in peril' ■

Miss Bell, the headmistress, said, 'Now girls, I want you to remember the fishermen at sea. The men who go out to sea, whatever the weather, to get fish for all of us to eat. These men risk their lives in gales and storms so that we may eat fish. So let us pray for them and their families. Everyone kneel.'

Joy thought to herself, 'I knew she would say that when I saw it was raining this morning.' All the girls in the lower senior school went down on their knees onto the wooden floor. 'I don't

mind praying, God,' said Joy, 'But it *do* make your knees hurt.'
'Now we will all say the Lord's Prayer out loud,' said Miss Bell,
interrupting Joy's prayer, so quickly Joy added, 'Keep the men
safe, God.' The girls chanted, 'Our Father.' When 'for ever and
ever, amen' was said, Miss Bell shouted; her voice was shaky and
sounded more like a scream, just like an aging soprano. It was
high in volume, but it lost its message to the girls so they rose to
their feet talking to each other. 'Be quiet, will you. This is a
morning service not a circus. Remember you are in the presence
of God!' Her voice then dropped to almost a whisper as she said,
'We will now sing for those in peril on the sea.' As Miss, the
music teacher, played the first bars of the hymn on the piano, the
girls and their teachers cleared their throats. What a noise; it
sounded like the gathering of the bronchial choral society!

Miss Bell, who was standing on the platform in the school hall,
was a thin woman. Her black hair streaked with grey was pulled
back into a bun at the back of her head. She wore grannie glasses
and a well-tailored black suit. Her shoes were lace-ups. Miss Bell
was dressed just as you would expect a headmistress would dress.
You could see she was preparing herself for the announcements
that were to come. Her arms started to wave about like a fairy
waving its wand. Up she went on tiptoe; she always did that when
there was something she was going to say which she considered
important. 'Settle down, settle down,' Miss Bell was away again,
screaming her head off. 'I want all of you girls to make a single
file past me, and you are to show me both sides of your hands as
you go by. You will start from the back of the hall. Will teachers
supervise the girls to make sure this is done in an orderly fashion
please.'

'What's she up to now?' Joy wondered. 'Something nasty you
can depend on that.' The girls began moving from their places,
teachers ushering the girls down the sides of the hall and across
the front of the platform. Each girl stretched out her arms and
showed Miss Bell the fronts and backs of her hands. Everyone in
the hall was paying attention, curious to know what this latest
game of the headmistress was all about.

It was Joy's turn to show her hands, which she did. Then Miss
Bell said, 'Let me see them again, child,' in a friendly way, her
eyes peering through her glasses which were perched on the end
of her nose. This Joy did. Then Miss Bell said to a puzzled Joy,
'Stand to one side.' Joy stood at the side of her headmistress. The
rest of the lower school showed their hands, but no one else was
made to stand to one side. What a fool Joy felt, standing there

exposed to the enquiring eyes of the girls; her head bowed so she could examine her hands, but Joy could find nothing wrong with them.

All the girls were now back in their places waiting for Miss Bell to reveal to them what was going to happen next. It was quite exciting for them.

'Now girls, it has come to my notice that you are coming to school with dirty hands and fingernails. So this morning I have looked at all your hands and nails, and there is only one girl here with clean hands and nails. That girl is Joyce Long.' Joy could have died with shame. Every girl and teacher was looking at her wide-eyed in amazement. Her heart was beating fast and she felt sick; never before had she been praised for anything in front of the school. Oh yes, she had been up there before, to be told off for playing truant from school and for answering the teachers back. That had been bad enough, but to be praised for keeping oneself clean seemed to Joy an insult.

Miss Bell continued yelling, 'To think there is only one girl in the whole of the first and second year with clean hands and nails. I think that is disgusting. From now on teachers will examine all your hands and nails before you start your school work. Now to show you what clean hands look like, Joyce Long will stand at the hall doors and will show her hands, both sides, to each girl as they leave the hall.' Turning to Joy she said, 'Come along Joyce dear,' in a sweet voice, then she smiled showing a horsy set of pure white, false teeth.

Joy had been battling with herself while Miss Bell had been yelling at the girls. She had been trying to throw off the humiliation she felt. Oh how she wished her hands were dirty. If only they were, she would be with all the girls where she belonged. Joy thought it was wrong of Miss Bell to use her in this way. She had to think quickly or she would from then on be isolated from the girls, which would mean she would lose all her friends. Miss Bell was making her different from the other girls; looking at the rows of girls Joy could feel the hostility coming from them. Joy smiled at the headmistress and walked to the hall door. Standing straight backed, she held out her hands, but as each girl looked at them, she mimicked Miss Bell waving her hands about. Joy looked at each girl wide-eyed and smiled with her top teeth over her bottom lip trying to look horsy like Miss Bell. The hostile look left the girls eyes and a look of merriment came into them.

When the last girl and teacher had gone only Joy and the headmistress were in the school hall. Miss Bell gave a weary sigh

and said in a tired voice, 'Go back to your classroom, Joyce.'
Joyce looked at Miss Bell and thought, 'She's quite old really.'

Pat Dallimore

■ The confirmation class ■

'Sister! Sister! Maureen O'Shea's knitting is lost. It's not in the
press, sister,' came a cry from the classroom. 'I'll look for it,'
said Kathleen, whose personality was a bit more wild than timid
Maureen's. Getting up from her desk, she walked up and stood
on the low window ledge in the hope of seeing the knitting buried
in the back of the press. Rising up on tip toes, she extended her
left leg for balance. She was fully engrossed in her search when
she heard the crash! Her head sprung around to see what had
happened, and there on the floor the huge statue of Our Blessed
Lady was in smithereens. In that split second she realized she had
kicked the piano with her outstretched leg, unbalancing the statue
that was unsteadily perched there, toppling it to the floor. She
knew it was an accident but when she saw the temper flashing in
Sr Monica's eyes, 'I'm sorry,' or, 'It was an accident,' seemed
quite irrelevant. 'Oh God!' she thought, 'What am I in for now?'

She was answered with six of the best on each hand with the
split bamboo and a litany of abuse hurled at her in front of all
her classmates. The sudden shock and injustice of it all levelled
her to compulsive sobbing in seconds and in that state she spent
the whole of the knitting class. Nearing the end of the class, Sr
Teresa came in to see Sr Monica whose temper quickly prompted
her to humiliate Kathleen even further, by relating to Sr Teresa
that, 'This hussy carelessly broke the statue.'

School over, Kathleen was relieved to leave the scene of the
accident. At home, she sat silently playing with her dinner, unable
to eat it as she was still full of emotion.

'Why aren't you eating your dinner?' her mother asked.

'I'm not hungry,' came the muffled reply.

'Why aren't you hungry? What's wrong with you? Your eyes
are all puffed; were you crying?'

The avalanche of questions brought the tears flooding again.

She had been worried about telling them at home about it because if she was wrong in some way that grown-ups see, then she would be punished twice. Her worries were unwarranted. The whole story came out between sobs until she was drained. Still unable to eat, she stayed around her mother long enough to be comforted and then, to her, the episode was over and off she went out to play.

Down the fields was where she played with her friends, spending almost all of her free time there, only coming home to eat and sleep, and if she could have avoided this she would have. There she was happy, lost in her world of friends, games and make-believe.

Today they weren't running as usual through the fields, but were all attentively listening to Helen describing in detail her confirmation dress. 'It's bright pink and you can see through the top skirt and when you twirl it goes out real wide, like a ballerina's tu-tu,' Helen explained with all of her being. A dress to be envied by all, Kathleen thought, and Helen must be really rich. She overheard her mother say once that Mr O'Brien, Helen's father, had a good, steady job, and what she would be able to do if she had a man's steady wage coming in. Kathleen knew that her dress was coming from the nuns. The sew-guild, organised by the nuns, made baby clothes and confirmation dresses that they gave to the poor. Her mother explained that the dresses were gorgeous and that she would be going down to the convent one day after school to be measured. Owning this dress would be fantastic, she thought, as she remembered her communion. She'd felt like the fairy princess on the fluffiest clouds until she had to take the borrowed dress off after the ceremony in case anything happened to it. And her coat, that big, pink coat off the bed, that Mrs. Brennan's sister cut down and turned for ten shillings, had been a success after all, but still, she would have preferred to take her chances on the weather without a coat and own the dress. This time she would own it, and it was private, being measured in the convent; she wouldn't have to explain it to anyone. The idea of wearing her confirmation dress every Sunday brought a flutter to her heart that banished any envy she had felt for Helen, and in that excited mood they headed for the poppy hill to unfold all the adventures it held.

Next morning she was early for school as usual as her mother had to get out to work. Her mother worked in the local food centre which ran dinners for poor pregnant women whose chances of a proper dinner every day were virtually nil. It also sold cheap, cooked foods to poor families in the area. This was run by a nun and four women. Kathleen had heard them at home discuss the pay as pittance, but her mother always protested that the hours and perks were marvellous. She could be out with the children to school in the morning and home with them again in the afternoon, and there was no denying that their eating habits had changed drastically since the job started. About half of the class were in when Sr Monica arrived and having settled for a minute she called: 'Kathleen Maguire, come up here, please.' Kathleen stopped chatting with her friends and walked up the long classroom a little apprehensively, wearing a quizzical look. Sr Monica produced a tape measure which made Kathleen's heart miss a beat and her face flush a deep crimson. 'This can't really be happening to me,' she thought and her eyes darted around her classmates for that dreaded reaction. With her little heart pounding furiously in her breast in full view of everyone, Sr Monica measured her for her confirmation dress. She tried desperately to display an air of uncaring arrogance to cover her humiliation, while she rushed her mind to make ready answers to the all-too-obvious questions from her schoolmates. In the end, she feigned ignorance of it. Ego shattered, she was incapable of any other defence under this pressure. During the rest of the day she wondered why Sr Monica singled her out to hate.

The weekend came and went, and in no time it was Monday morning again. Sr Monica's first remarks of the morning were: 'Kathleen Maguire, the Head Nun would like to see you in her office.' Kathleen just felt her stomach drop and her face flush, as she wondered what mischief she had done that merited such recognition from the Head Nun. Mentally she reviewed all her normal mischief, which included walking the school railings or climbing over the wire fence at the back, but it must be a lot worse than that. As it turned out, her father had met Sr Monica and candidly aired his views on punishments for statue breaking, so now she had to pay for telling her mother about it. 'And we don't all go home telling our parents every little thing that happens, like babies in the junior classes,' the Head Nun went on.

Silenced and scared she was, but what they couldn't take back was her beautiful, powder-blue dress with the tiny, velvet-like spots on. She loved the satin bow which sat under the tiny collar at the neck and had two ribbons streaming down from it. She was a Sunday Cinderella or Snow White every Sunday, when she wore her confirmation dress with great pride.

Carmel Jennings

■ 'D for Dad' ■

Ellen sat on the great, stone ball on top of the gatepost and looked at the garden. It was large and wild and still bore traces of the garden it must once have been. Her mother often remarked guiltily that they ought to 'Dig for Victory', but she never explained how that would help win the war. What was the fuss about? As soon as dad came home he would be able to see to it all.

At the back of her mind was a memory of her father from his last leave as a very tall, brown man in khaki battledress, but the vivid picture of him that had at first remained was beginning to blur around the edges as the months wore on; and sometimes she could not remember his face at all and would have to go to her mother's bedroom to look at his framed photograph. He had carried her on his shoulders past Marks and Spencer's, and Joyce Williams had seen her and was jealous because of his uniform.

From her vantage point, she could see the new baby in his blanket cocoon, lying in her old, black pram on the terrace. The house windows were opened as far as the old frames would allow so that her mother could hear his mandatory wails instantly. He was a nice baby but rather boring. He slept, fed and sucked his thumb; and the only entertainment he offered was at bath-time when she was allowed to sprinkle him with talc and pass the giant safety pins. Perhaps, when he was older, he would become more exciting.

Mam came out onto the terrace now to look at the baby. It was nearly tea-time and Ellen did not want to go indoors just yet so she slowly slid down behind the gatepost. She hung by her fingertips until she was at full stretch, and then allowed herself to drop the rest of the way. As she was doing it, she heard her mother call, and, not sure whether she had been seen, she slipped off her sandals and paddled into the stream, ducking into the semidarkness of the culvert which carried the water under the road. It was a hiding-place that she had used many times before. She stood quite still, listening to her mother, who had come down to the gate, calling her name over and over again, until she got tired and went back up the path clucking like a vexed hen.

The little girl giggled softly to herself. Best to wait here for a few seconds just to make sure she had gone. It was a funny sensation, curling her bare toes around the tiny, polished stones on the stream bed. The water, straight from the hills, was ice-cold and numbed her feet. It gurgled and echoed, deep and hollow.

Feathery green slime, struggling to free itself from its rocky base, snaked about her ankles.

After a bit, she came out through the bright semicircle of light and sat on the bank to replace her sandals, thinking what to do next. Then she went around the side of the garden wall until she came to a place where the footholds were easy and numerous and she would be hidden from the house by the trees as she climbed over into the garden.

The battered plank door of the chicken-coop complained bitterly as Ellen forced it open. It refused to go more than halfway and stood askew on its one remaining hinge. Inside, the dry, sharp smell of dust made her want to sneeze. Spiders had been busy embellishing the corners, and there were mouse-droppings on the floor. She made a mental note to clean the place out again at the first opportunity, but right now it was not very inviting. She might as well go up to the house. At least she would avoid trouble that way.

Tea was the usual miserable affair. Ellen's mother, between bouts of shovelling pap into the baby, nagged on and on. Her sister, Bernadette, had come home from the munitions factory and sat opposite her, listlessly picking at an egg salad.

'She must have seen me. I don't know how she managed to run so fast. I went straight down to the gate and there was no sign of her.'

Ellen looked down at her plate and counted the stones from the tinned plums.

'Anyway, she must have heard me calling.'

'Little menace,' said Bernie. 'I hate having to go anywhere with her. She doesn't know how to behave. She ruined the toes of her shoes yesterday, kicking at stones in the road like a boy.'

Ellen fingered her right upper arm, which was still bruised from Bernie's restraining grip as they had walked home from chapel. Bernie would smile sweetly at people as they passed, and all the time her hard fingers were digging into Ellen's flesh.

'Well, *did* you hear me?'

'Yes.'

'Then why didn't you come? I've got more to do than to keep running after you, you know. Oh! I wish your father were home – he'd soon sort you out. You're more trouble to me than Bernadette ever was. I never saw such a difference in two girls.'

Something very like a smirk appeared on her sister's face.

'Well, if you've finished your tea you can get up to your room. Perhaps next time you hear me call you'll remember that it doesn't

49

pay not to come.'

He wouldn't sort her out: he would understand why she wanted to stay out a bit longer in the sun. They didn't know anything, those two. She slipped quietly off her chair. There was no point in arguing. Whatever she did was wrong. They seemed set on making her life a misery.

Once in her room she passed the time by picking at the plaster in the wall behind the bedhead. Already she had got through to the laths and, if she could make a hole big enough to get an arm through, she thought she might find hidden treasure. Perhaps someone who had lived in the house long ago had hidden all his worldly possessions there in that very spot and then died a horrible, sudden death, his last words frozen on his tortured lips.

It would be best if the treasure were money. Jewellery was no good. She didn't need jewellery. But she could use money to buy ever such a lot of useful things: a bike, of course, a red one with a lamp and a bell and a white bag on the back. She would buy a carpet and a new frock for her mother and a silver mug for the baby, but she wouldn't get Bernie anything. She'd let her come on holiday with them though, just so that she could help to mind the baby. They could go to an hotel in Barry and spend a whole week near the sea, not just a day, like on the Sunday School outing.

When she was tired of picking plaster she got out a copy of 'Sunny Stories' and a stub of candle that she kept under a loose floorboard. Her mother had removed the electric light bulb because there were no blackout curtains in her room, but the light from the candle was only faint, and if she put it down on the floor and lay on the rag rug behind the bed and away from the window, it should be alright. She had smuggled up some matches in the pocket of her navy blue knickers.

She settled down comfortably with a pillow under her tummy, and her shadow rose and fell on the wall as the candle flickered in the draught. The shadow suddenly jumped across the ceiling as a series of loud bangs on the front door echoed through the house.

'Put that ruddy light out!'

There was panic downstairs, and the noise of running feet and the opening of doors competed with the continuing bangs.

She snuffed the candle with wet fingers, stuffed the book under the mattress and dived under the bedclothes as her mother came running up the stairs.

'What do you think you're doing?'

'Wha – whassamarrer? Is it morning?'

'Don't you try that with me – I can smell the candlegrease. You wait, young lady. We'll see about this in a minute.'

Her mother clattered back downstairs and she heard her placating the Air Raid Warden. His voice was now low and gruff. He didn't sound so angry any more, but although she couldn't hear the words, he didn't sound pleased either. She sat up, trembling in the dark and listened to his footsteps echoing down the path and away into the night.

Ellen suffered her mother's furious tirade in silence and only after she had gone did she allow herself to cry. There was to be no pocket-money for a month, and that meant she wouldn't be able to go to Saturday morning pictures at Bethesda chapel. There was nothing to look forward to any more. Life just wasn't worth living. She hated her mother almost as much as she hated Bernie. Well, she'd show them! She dried her tears and made her plans. As soon as they were both safely in bed she was going to run away. When they found her bed empty in the morning they'd realize just how cruel they were. She would lie awake and wait for them both to come to bed, wait a bit for them to go to sleep and then she would creep down and sneak away.

She awoke suddenly, annoyed with herself. The room was black except for a moving picture of leaves projected by the moonlight onto the window-facing wall, and she had no idea of the time.

The ancient bed-springs moaned painfully at being disturbed as she slithered out from under the sheets and felt the cool lino with her bare toes. Carefully, she eased open the creaking door and went out onto the landing. There was a pencil of light showing under the kitchen door. It was not so late. A chair screeched across the floor downstairs and she jumped back into the shadows as the door was opened and a dazzle of light threw the bannisters into relief, just where she had been leaning over. Bernie stood in the doorway, one hand on the doorknob, looking back into the room, laughing and talking softly. Her mother said something inaudible and then Bernie called goodnight, shutting the door.

Ellen glided stealthily back into the shadowy bedroom and stood listening with her ear to the crack as her sister came up the stairs. She did not bother to look in to see if Ellen were awake and the girl was relieved and annoyed at the same time. When Bernie had shut her bedroom door behind her, she prudently got back into bed to wait for her mother to come up.

Before long she heard her crossing the hall to check the bolts on the front door and then the creak of the stairs – a loud squeak on the second stair from the top – and then she was standing beside the bed, smoothing back the hair from her forehead in the dark.

'Ellen are you awake?'

Carefully, she kept her breathing deep and regular, stirring slightly as if disturbed in sleep. Her mother gently brushed her lips against her cheek, and Ellen felt a pang of conscience but she continued to lie there, waiting for her mother to go away.

When she had gone it seemed a long time, lying there listening to the night noises, making sure that everyone was asleep before she got up again.

As she crept downstairs the baby whimpered in his sleep but did not wake. She took what she needed from the kitchen and was about to let herself out when her mother's door opened.

'Who's there?'

Ellen held her breath and shrank back against the wall, perfectly still. There was no sound but the beating of her heart. Her mother's shadow grew large on the stair wall as she leaned over the bannister, and then Ellen heard her mother mutter to herself and the shadow shrank and disappeared as the bedroom door shut. She stayed exactly as she was for a long time and then, slowly and carefully, without making a sound, she drew back the bolts.

As she opened the front door a miracle happened. First she was aware of a loud droning noise like a million bees, and then she looked up to see the sky alive with moving stars. As she stared she made out shapes. Each star was attached to a plane. There were Spitfires and Hurricanes and some she didn't know, and they all had their lights on! Wave after wave passed overhead and suddenly all the valley below was alive with answering lights as doors and windows were flung open with a total disregard for black-out regulations. And still they came. Ellen had never seen a night lit up like this one. It was a whole new world.

The hall light had been switched on behind her and her mother was standing there screaming with delight. Bernadette had switched the wireless on, loud.

'What is it?' shrieked Ellen.

'It's D-day!' Bernie shouted back.

'What does it mean?'

'It means the war will be over soon, and we're going to win, that's what it means.'

'D for Dad,' said Ellen.

She watched until the last light had gone from the valley and then she let Bernie take her by the hand and lead her back upstairs. They all slept together in the big bed that night, Ellen sandwiched cosily between her sister and mother.

Beth Edge

■ Letting go ■

Both girls smiled at Monica from across the damp road.

'Why don't you put your umbrellas up?'

Each teenager gave a knowing, slightly embarrassed look to the other. Monica's daughter smiled and cockily answered: 'It's only a bit of rain.'

'Where are you going?' Monica asked.

The two girls looked at each other, gave that smile, and her daughter replied: 'Oh, just out, I'll be back for half-past nine.'

'Think on then, 'cause I'll be back for nine-thirty too.'

Both girls looked across at Monica as she put her umbrella up. Immediately they burst out laughing. Monica smiled then shouted: 'Why y're laughing?'

'Have you seen the sight of your umbrella?'

'What's up with it?'

'Look at it, it's broken.'

'It's not bad, keeps the rain off. Do you want to borrow it?'

The girls smiled and burst out laughing. As Monica was walking away they shouted, 'Wouldn't be seen dead with that umbrella.'

Monica smiled to herself as the girls passed on. Her umbrella only needed two bits of material fastening onto the spikes. but this mattered to them.

She felt a gap growing between her daughter and herself, yet she had enjoyed seeing her with her friend, seeing that youthful vitality brim full. But as Monica walked to her evening class she began to visualise her daughter's face. As the picture became clearer, she saw that her daughter was wearing make-up. 'Well, that's youth, they've got to try things out. But why make-up? Well, she's fourteen, lads will come into her life now.'

Monica really enjoyed the evening class and what made it more enjoyable was that she could go out now and leave her child – teenager – without feeling anxious and then guilty. It was the beginning of a new freedom for her. Even other nights she could go out now to see her friends or to go to the community school meetings that she was beginning to enjoy being involved in.

As Monica returned home, she noticed that there weren't any lights on in the house and her daughter left lights on as though it was Blackpool illuminations. Anxiety began to creep through her as she found all the rooms empty. Fears for her child shuffled through her mind. She didn't mind her daughter being a bit late. Remembrances of her own teenage years came back to her. Nearly always late home. Always the questions: 'Where've you been? You're late', and always the excuses. Her Carlton days: shocking-pink layered net underskirt, pink skirt and bright green ankle socks; jiving with girls to Buddy Holly's music, but always with an eye somewhere else. Talking to her girlfriends, yet waiting for something: that waiting was a transition, a gap between childhood and youth. The something became clearer to Monica, it was a part of the waiting, in transition to the something, boys. Was her daughter ready for this?

A fiddling, a key. The front door opening. Her daughter entering the room, all vibrant. Fears slithered from Monica's mind.

'You're a bit late, luv.'

'Oh, me and Sue walked back from Alison's.'

'Well, try not to be late again. I get a bit worried for you.'

After supper was over and her daughter had gone to bed, Monica pondered over her daughter's reason for being late. Was she seeing lads? Monica didn't like this at all. Her daughter might not have been at Alison's, might even have been with lads. Yet Monica accepted her daughter living her own life. 'She's a teenager, she should have some freedom, just like me.' But Monica did not like these strange feelings. Perhaps she should insist that her daughter be home for a certain time. And should she find out who the friend was? No, she didn't like that. It was prying into her daughter's personal life, a life that her daughter was starting to live. She must trust her. But still . . .

Early summer with light, warm evenings. Monica loved these long evenings in the garden. She loved looking at, and tending, her plants that she had grown from seed. She watched them thriving, stretching themselves into the air, their stems and leaves haughtily, healthily green. She passed by these to the flowers. Her young lupins that she'd grown from seed three years ago glowed pink and deep blue, full of vitality in their flower. She felt so pleased and satisfied with herself. It was demanding work growing plants, but it was worth it for her to see them thrive.

The evening began to cool slightly as dusk filtered the air. It was peaceful, just lingering there at the start of dusk. Minutes passed. Monica stirred herself, looked around and gathered up her gardening tools. Quite satisfied with herself, she went into the kitchen, unscrewed the top of a bottle of damson wine, poured herself a glass and sat down in an easy chair in the living room. She sipped at the wine, lingering over each sip until she began to feel uncomfortable. Surely it was getting late. It must be ten-thirty by now, and her daughter not back yet. It dawned on Monica that her daughter had said she was going roller skating with her friend Sue. Monica searched for a clock. Twenty to eleven, it's too late for her to be out. She hoped that nothing had happened. But she began to get worried. She forgot her wine and stood looking out of the window, out onto the street, then at the clock. Five minutes had passed by, but it seemed ages. Monica turned and walked away from the window. She didn't want to be seen watching for her daughter to come home, it didn't seem to be fair somehow.

Another five minutes gone, Monica sat in the chair drinking. She looked up through the window onto the street and saw her. Her fears subsided as relief flooded through her. Her daughter came into the room, looking bright, full of youth.

'You're late tonight. I was so worried. Why are you so late?'

'Me and Sue went to the chippy and then walked back with some friends.'

'Who were the friends?'

'Oh, just some friends from the roller rink.'

Monica dreaded this, but asked, 'Were there some lads?'

Her daughter looked at her with a half-concealed smile and questioning glance. 'There may have been.'

'I do get worried for you, you know. I wouldn't like anything to happen to you.'

'But mum, I can look after myself. I'm not stupid. I'll try to be earlier next time.'

Monica smiled at her daughter, looked at her young, lithe body in the fitted denim jeans. Her eyes moved up to her tee shirt, onto her daughter's small breasts, then to her lightly made-up face, her brown sparkling eyes. Yes, her daughter was growing up. Jo looked at her mother, smiled and passed by into the kitchen.

More damson wine and hours later into the night, Monica sat

there thinking. She loved those moments in the evening, seldom now though, when her daughter came and sat on the settee with her. They'd talk, her daughter would nestle up to her. Monica's arm would stretch onto her daughter's shoulder and her fingers would start playing with her hair. But a cold, hard feeling hurt Monica now. 'What if a lad had done that to Jo, and Jo had accepted it, liked it even?' That couldn't be. Not her daughter. It was painful for Monica, she'd never thought of this before. But her daughter was growing up. 'Why shouldn't Jo want this?' She was the same as other girls. It hurt Monica, though, to see a picture of a lad's arm over the shoulder of her daughter. She fought on through the pain, saw sex, dismissed it, realising her daughter wasn't ready for this yet. Monica now saw Jo as she had seen her tonight, vibrantly testing, tasting, exploring her own personal life. 'That must be,' Monica thought. One day, sometime, she knew that Jo would talk about lads as well as girls. She'd have to accept it and wait for that something to happen.

Bernadette Tweedale

■ A visitor ■

Jessie sat, the rasp of the metal on the file beginning to get on her nerves. 'Cum on,' she muttered. 'Friggin' thing! The kids 'll be in soon an' ther's no dinner ready . . . dinner!' she snorted. 'Nice dinner it is an' all . . . porrage.'

She stood up. 'There! That should do it.' Gathering the pinny with the metal bits in, she shook it in the hearth and went into the kitchen. Putting the halfpenny in the gas meter, she turned the dial and down it dropped. She lighted the gas thinking, 'I'm getting quite a dab hand at that filing. I wunder, cud I gerra job at it? Mind you, I don't suppose the Gas Company'd take me on.'

She started to tidy around and get the dinner ready. The kitchen door opened, and in came Davey, her youngest, covered in soot.

'Mam, I fell over.'

'My Jezus,' Jessie said, 'Ow did ya manage that? I've told ya till I'm blue in face ta keepaway frum that oller. I'll bleedin' kill that sweep anyway when I see him. He's got no right to throw ya in there.' Pulling Davey's clothes off, Jessie gave him a smack. 'You can't do as ya told. Well, ya'll have ta stay in 'cos I've got no more clothes dry for ya.'

Davey was screaming. 'I couldn't help it. I fell over,' he sobbed.

'Alright, alright! I didn't hit ya tha'ard. You'd think you'd had ya leg off. Keep still, will ya, while I wash ya.'

Dave screamed louder. 'But I've already been washed once.'

'Ya can't go round like that, ya look like Al Jolson. There ya dun. Now go an' sit be the fire. The others'll be in in a minute.'

Soon the rest of the kids were home. Frankie, at thirteen the eldest, then Mary, Johnnie . . . and Davey you've met. The man of the house, Frank senior, was at work on the building. He wouldn't be home till about eight or nine, depending on his pocket and how many pints he could get down in comfort.

The kids were busy hanging up wet stockings on the mantelpiece and drying their heads, having been caught in a sudden downpour.

'Oh aye, Mam, whenner we getting our dinner? I'm starving.' This from Johnnie.

'Just a minute, just a minute. Let's get ya head dried before you catch cold.' Jessie rubbed away at Johnnie's hair. 'Mary, did ya get that seven an six off ya Aunty Rose?'

'Yes, Mam,' Mary said. 'Here it is. An' Rose says she wants it back first thing Friday morning and not to ask again 'cos that's all she's got, an' I'm not going there any more. I hate her. So don't ever ask me again.'

'What did she say this time?' asked Jessie.

'Oh, ya know, about me Dar being drunk an' has been fighting again.'

'That'll do,' Jessie said. 'Your Aunt Rose means well. She can't help being nosey an' we'd be a lot worse off if it wasn't for her.'

'Oh aye, Mam, give us our dinner will ya?' Johnnie said. 'What is it, anyway?'

Jessie looked at them. 'Porrage,' she said.

'Porrage!' A cry of horror from the kids. 'I hate porrage' came as if with one voice. For once they agreed about something.

'Well, that's all there is so them that wants it can have it an' those that don't can do without'

'Why can't we have chips now?' Frankie said.

'Don't ya be so bleedin' arf faced,' replied Jessie. 'An' get that ate.'

Just then the door opened and who walked in, only Father

Mullin.

'Oh, hello Father,' she said. 'Ooh, I hope he didn't hear me,' she thought.

'Hello Father,' said the kids, standing up.

'Hello, and how are we all? Well, I hope.'

'Yes, Father,' they chorused.

'Don't let me keep you from your dinner, children. Carry on now before it gets cold.'

'Well, it's only porrage, Father,' a redfaced Jessie explained. 'Today's a bad day.'

'And what's wrong with porrage? A good nourishing meal an' all, it is. Just the thing on a day like this. It'll do them the world of good'.

'How would ya know, ya big fat get?' thought Johnnie, lowering his head for fear the priest would see him glaring. 'I bet you don't have ta eat porrage for your dinner. No, I bet ya get steak an' kidney pies or bacon and eggs.' These being his favourite meals, the thought of the priest having them didn't make the porrage go down any easier.

'Hmm, and all attending Holy Mass, I hope, and receiving the sacraments,' the priest said.

'Yes, Father,' they chorused.

'And you, Mrs. James?'

'Oh yes, Father,' Jessie replied, thinking, 'God forgive the liar, but it's hard to attend Mass when you can't afford the collection.'

'And now to business,' said Father Mullin.

'Please God, don't let it be a collection,' Jessie looked at the three half-crowns on the table. 'Oh God,' she prayed, 'you couldn't be that bad.'

'Well, as you know,' continued the priest, 'we're having a mission next week and there'll be certain streets in which we gather to pray so that everyone can join in. This is one of them and we'll want to put an altar outside your door if it wouldn't be too much trouble'.

'Oh no trouble at all, Father. About what time would it be?' said Jessie thinking, 'I'd better warn Frank to stay away. I don't want him coming here from The Throstles with his ale in him, making a show of us.'

'Eight-thirty, I think. That's about the best time, Mrs. James. I'll just give you a blessing now.' Making the sign of the cross, he said, 'In nomine Patris et Filii et Spiritus Sancti, Amen.'

'Amen,' they replied.

'Good day now.'

'Goodbye Father.'

Jessie looked around and smiled, 'Well, I'll have to send for Father Mullin next time we have porrage. That's the first time ya've eaten it all.'

Ellen Richardson

■ Death came to dinner ■

She straightened the cards; halfway through Christmas day and all was well! She couldn't believe it; something had to go wrong, it always did. Bert was in the kitchen serving up dinner. Bless him; every year without fail he took over the cooking. It was his regular 'gift' to her. How many wives were that lucky?

Watching the kids glued to the telly she felt relaxed, enjoying the calm. No, it couldn't last. But, after the bedlam of the morning, the shrieks and squeals of delight as they uncovered each present, the paper, labels, boxes, the lot making the room look like a battlefield, the calm felt like the cease-fire in a war.

It didn't last long. There was a knock on the door breaking the silence.

'For Heaven's sake, one of you answer it.' Strange how the children went deaf when watching a cartoon! The next-door neighbour walked in.

'Can I have a word with you, Ethel?'

'Sure, would you like a drink?' Any other day it would have been, 'I'll make you a cuppa,' but today was special. 'Having a nice time, Mary?'

'Not really,' Mary said, looking uneasy. 'I know I shouldn't trouble you just now but could you come and look at the old lady down the street? I've just been in and I don't like the look of her.'

As they walked the few yards down the street, Ethel asked the question that had been puzzling her.

'How did you get in if she's ill?'

'The door was open,' Mary still looked worried. 'I don't like to go to the bed on my own. It's in the living room, and she looked so ill, I just ran for you.'

59

As Ethel went to the bedside, Mary stayed, as she had done before, in the doorway.

'You had better phone for the doctor, if you can find one, if not, get the police. They will know what to do.' Ethel took control. 'It looks like that illness you know, that one caused by the cold. Hypo— something. There was an article in the papers about it. Go on, hurry up.' Mary was off like a shot, only too glad to get away.

'First things first,' Ethel thought. 'Get the room warm.' She bent down to turn on the fire. 'Damn!' The blasted thing wouldn't work. She turned back to the bed. Gently she tried to massage the thin, bony arm that lay across the covers. 'God!' She was cold. 'It must have been like a fridge in here. Poor soul. Fancy being ill and alone on Christmas Day.' Ethel looked around the room. Whoever the woman was, she certainly wasn't friendless. There were greeting cards everywhere. She looked again at the old woman. Slowly she took the poor, wizened hand and eased it back under the blankets. She pulled the bedclothes up around her wrinkled neck. Did she look a bit warmer? There seemed to be some colour coming back to her face.

'I wonder if she has any relatives?' Nervously, Ethel started to read the cards, but it was a waste of time. Only Christian names. She sat by the bed and lit a cigarette. Who was it said they calmed the nerves? The old lady had obviously been enjoying herself. There was a half-empty box of chocolates and a cup of cold tea on the bedside table. She pushed them back, away from the edge. She jumped up as she heard the door close. Help at last. Not before time either!

The police were casual, almost callous, but it was probably an everyday occurrence to them. A quick glance at the bed and one said to the other. 'You had better radio in, Brian.'

'OK, Jack.'

That was that. Brian disappeared. Jack walked to the other side of the bed. Ethel wondered why; you could see all there was to see at this side.

Suddenly he spoke, 'Have you touched anything?'

'No. Well, not really.' It was Ethel's turn to feel uneasy. What was he getting at? 'She will be alright, won't she?'

Jack ignored that. 'Not really? Either you did or you didn't. Which?'

'Well, I touched the fire when I tried to light it. Oh, I moved the chocolates and the cup.' Ethel was downright frightened by now.

'Nothing else? You're sure?' Jack said.

'Only the cards. I thought I might find someone to get in touch with.'

There was a pause. 'You didn't come to this side of the bed at all?' Jack was certainly asking some funny questions.

'No! Why should I?' she said. 'I can see the old lady from here. You are getting at something. What?' Anger was taking over from fear. He had no right to treat her like this.

'I am getting at this.' He held up an old-fashioned handbag. 'It's empty. Know anything about it?' She had to be dreaming! This was a nightmare! She couldn't possibly be accused of stealing, could she? That only happened in films, in papers, it did not happen to ordinary folk.

Brian came back. 'We can get off now, Jack. It's all been taken care of. The old woman died twelve hours ago. The station already knew. It was reported by the doctor this morning. They have taken her papers and pension book.'

Jack put his cap back on. 'That solves the mystery of the empty bag.'

Ethel took a deep breath. How dare they shrug it off like that! 'Why, if everyone knew about it, was the door left open for us to walk in like that?' She almost screamed the question at Brian.

'It was left open so that the body could be collected,' he muttered, almost sheepishly. 'You can go home now, ladies.'

As they stepped outside, Ethel suddenly felt faint. 'Are you alright missus?' Jack became almost human. Alright? When she had been questioned like a criminal, practically accused of being a thief and had spent the last half an hour trying to warm the body of a corpse! The thought of that made her go cold. Strange sense of humour Jack had!

Mary took her arm. 'Come on love, let's go back.' In silence they walked up the street. There was nothing to be said. Not yet, not now.

Bert was waiting for her. 'The children have eaten, but I waited for you.' How could she tell him that she wouldn't eat it, when he had worked so hard?

The phone rang. 'It's for you Mum, long distance.'

Only half-aware of what was said, the significance of 'long distance' didn't dawn on her. Only when she heard her married daughter's voice did she realise the call was from Germany.

'Terry and I have just been talking about the rotten Christmas you had last year when Auntie Florrie died, and the year before, when Uncle Bob was very ill, so we said, "Hang the expense."

We've rung you up to wish you a Happy Christmas.'

Just in time, Ethel remembered to say, 'The same to you,' as she hung up.

The youngest child was waiting. 'I've got the wishbone. Will you pull it with me?' Ethel pulled and she wished – oh how she wished! Next year, perhaps, a merry Christmas . . .?

Doris Sydenham

■ Thank Gawd for the National Health ■

'5.45 appointment Mrs Symmons,' the efficient voice at the other end of the phone had said.

Lillian looked nervously down at her watch. It was now 5.15 and out of the corner of her eye she could see the pile of dirty dishes still waiting for her.

'Mum, come on, you're not helping. It's got to be finished for tomorrow. Everyone else will have theirs done, I bet they get help at home,' Paul whined accusingly.

She forced herself to concentrate on the map they were making of the route between their house and Paul's school.

'Oh Mum, no. That's not where the telephone box is, the postbox is there.'

At the same time as trying to remember details for the map, she was mentally making a note of what she still had to do before she was able to leave the house.

She had to clear up before Sue arrived, and Samantha still had to be got ready for bed; it would have to be a flannel over hands and face job tonight.

'Is that it? It's not very good; I bet it doesn't get put on the wall,' Paul complained as Lillian left the table.

'Typical,' she thought. Miss Fernado was a conscientious teacher, but she would pick tonight to ask them all to do maps.

In between doing the dishes she checked that Paul had all he needed for the cubs that night.

'Mummy, can I have a story before bed?' Samantha pleaded.

'Sorry love, not tonight, perhaps Sue will read you one when she arrives.'

'Some hopes,' she thought. Sue would either arrive with a pile of records or a man. Quickly, she packed Samantha off to bed, silently praying, 'Sam, please don't make a scene tonight.'

At 5.30 she hastily ran the comb through her hair and picked up her bag. 'Blast that Sue, where was she?'

'Mum, Sue's here,' Paul called.

Lillian heaved a sigh of relief. Running down the stairs, she heard the phone go.

'It's for you, it's Mum,' Sue laughed, seeing Lillian's perplexed face.

'Hello, Mum.'

'Hello dear, I wondered how things were, as you haven't rung for a couple of days.'

'No, I'm sorry Mum, I've been really busy. Look I've got to dash, I've got an appointment at the doctor's . . .'

'You not well?' her mother's anxious voice broke in.

'No, it's nothing to worry about . . . look Mum, I'll phone you tomorrow.'

She almost put the phone down while her mother dithered around deciding when was the best time for her to phone.

As she rushed down the road, she noticed it was drizzling; too bad, she hadn't time to go back for her umbrella.

'Blast, damn,' she said aloud as she saw the 143 disappear down the road. She looked at her watch, ten minutes to go. Another 143 might take ages to come; she'd better walk.

She arrived out of breath but on time.

'Go upstairs and wait, Mrs Symmons.'

She looked round the waiting room in dismay. One side for Dr Carn, and the other for Dr Drake. She had deliberately chosen Dr Drake because he was the quicker, but six people were sitting there.

'Are you waiting for Dr Drake?' she asked.

The waiting room was so quiet a pin could have been heard to drop. They all looked embarrassed at the fact that she had dared to speak in such a holy atmosphere. She gathered from the nods they were waiting for Dr Drake and sat down.

She should have known better. This appointment system didn't work. She didn't know why they bothered with it.

She looked round the room. Everyone sat in stiff upright positions. As the buzzer went, they looked as though they were being summoned to their execution.

63

The posters on the wall didn't help the atmosphere. Do clean your teeth regularly, don't overeat, do get the kids vaccinated, do use contraception and do make sure you are regular. The greyish coloured walls and scruffy linoleum added to the picture of total gloom.

In desperation she picked up a magazine, yellow with age, and tried to concentrate on imagining herself on the golden beach, a stone lighter and wearing the bikini the girl in the ad was wearing. She wondered why she always got butterflies in her stomach before seeing the doctor.

Then she arrived. You could hear her clomping up the stairs, breathing heavily, before she flung the door open. She knew as soon as she saw the massive woman that she was a talker.

'Please don't come and sit next to me,' she thought, but knew she would. 'They always smell me out,' she thought.

'Is this side for Dr Drake?' Her voice boomed throughout the room.

Lillian knew that she needn't reply, it was merely the woman's opening remarks for a whole dissertation that was about to follow.

'You been to Dr Drake before?' Not waiting for a reply she continued. 'He's alright, I suppose, not as good as Dr Jason, now she was a real lady, really bothered about you, until *he* died, she was never the same again.'

Lillian was aware of the fact that although everyone was pretending not to have seen the woman, all eyes were really on them, waiting to see how Lillian would respond under this pressure.

'Him,' the big woman gestured to Dr Carn's corner, 'he's all right but he's an Indian.' She sat back contented, as though pointing out his race had said it all. Lillian felt her face getting hotter as she buried her head more deeply in the magazine. She daren't look up at the others in the waiting room, especially at the Asian family sitting there.

To her relief the buzzer went. As she jumped up, so did the fat lady.

'No, I'm before you dear, I saw the nurse first with a urine specimen.'

What could she say? She had no intention of doing battle with this enormous lady. Silently she sat back in her chair. It was not quite 6.15pm. She thought of the pile of ironing that had to be done. She really must not be late for work tomorrow; she'd been late already once that week.

Feeling like a kid going for an interview for her first job, she knocked nervously on the doctor's door.

Dr Drake did not look up as she entered. She had never learnt what one was supposed to do on entering a doctor's room. Should she cough to catch his attention, say good evening as soon as entering, or what? The gap between his door and desk seemed enormous; she was almost tempted to curtsey.

'Name?'

She answered quietly.

'Well, Mrs. Symmons what can I do for you?' He was still writing.

She drew a deep breath. 'Well, doctor, I have been feeling so tired lately . . .'

For a brief moment his eyes looked at her above the glasses perched on the end of his nose, then he continued writing.

'You've been overdoing it, I expect. It's the time of year most people get run down, I'll give you a tonic. You should have a holiday.'

That's a joke she thought. It took her utmost strength to continue.

'But it's not just that, Doctor. I have this pain down here and I feel so ill at certain times of the month.'

He seemed relieved that she had added the last part of the sentence.

'I am afraid that's one of the crosses you women have to bear. I'll give you some pills to relieve the tension.'

Lillian realised she was being dismissed. She thought of all the people he had to see in one evening, how ill some of them looked in the waiting room; by comparison her complaint seemed so trivial. She probably was neurotic.

'Thank you, Doctor,' she said meekly, as he handed her the prescription.

Outside she felt exhilarated. She had made the effort of going to the Doctor and he didn't seem worried; he was the professional; he must know what he was doing.

If only she did not feel so tired. The rain was now falling quite heavily. As she approached the bus stop, she groaned.

Standing at the stop, there was no way of mistaking her, was the enormous lady.

'We've just missed one,' she greeted her. 'It'll be a long wait at this time of the night.'

'Alright, are you?'

Lillian nodded.

'Yes, they know what there're doing really, I keep telling Ted, go to the doctors, I've got faith in them, thank Gawd for the National Health.'

Lillian suddenly felt the sharp pain again. She was feeling too ill to do anything but quietly acquiesce.

Laureen Hickey

■ First steps to the last ■

It was cold. Even in his dreams he felt the cold. It was like a dull pain that took all the depth out of sleeping. You'd have thought having four in the same bed would have added a little warmth. Maybe it did. Jimmy couldn't tell, never having slept alone. The sound of his mother's voice pulled him, unwillingly, to complete wakefulness. She was shouting to Meggie, the woman upstairs, who owned a clock, asking what the time was.

Jimmy, at seven, was the youngest in the family. If that meant that all his clothes were hand me downs at least they never disappeared to the pawnshop as his brother Jack's long trousers had. Jack had started work as a rivet catcher in the shipyards and been bought his first pair of long trousers to mark the occasion. He'd been in the job, and trousers, just three days when Jimmy had come down with a fever. The last thing Jimmy remembered clearly was his mother and grandmother talking about scarlet fever. He'd heard that, if you had scarlet fever, your skin came off. As his temperature rose he was convinced large chunks of flesh were about to fall from his bones.

Jack's trousers went to the pawnbroker's and, when their mother had the money, the doctor was called. After Jimmy had been examined the doctor clicked his little bag shut and, standing up, smiled. It wasn't scarlet fever, just 'something going round'. He was paid and clinked the precious coins together absent-mindedly in his pocket as he left. His parting words were, 'Keep him warm and if you give him as much hot broth as he can keep down, he'll be fine.'

If the 'broth' was often the clearest soup it still did the trick.

Jimmy recovered in ten days. Jack though, didn't get his trousers back for three weeks and, after that, made sure they couldn't disappear again without his knowing by sleeping with them under his side of the flock mattress. Jack was fourteen. When Jimmy was fourteen he'd get a job and a pair of long trousers.

The Monday morning that Jimmy was due to go back to school the snow was barely three inches deep. Jimmy though, feet softened by almost a fortnight in bed, dreaded the walk to school. For the first time, he began to envy people who had boots or shoes. It didn't matter that his short pants had a large patch in the seat, that his shirt was one of his dad's cut down or that his jersey had no elbows. The shoes did matter, as he admitted to his brother Joe, who was two years his elder. Joe, a tall, thin, cheerful lad with corn-coloured hair, had never minded going barefoot. He laughed, 'You've got to be kidding, our Jimmy. Look at Bobby, he's got boots. You want to be like Bobby?'

Bobby lived opposite and had been given a pair of boots for Christmas by his uncle, a sailor. His mother would lean out of her second floor window as soon as Bobby left the house and shout, 'You mind what you're doing with them new boots on,' so the whole street could hear. She'd be there again when he came home with the same message. Soon Bobby had a retinue of boys whenever he went out. 'You mind what you're doing with them new boots on,' they'd chant until one of them got within kicking distance of the boots.

Jimmy never got the chance to say whether he'd like to be like Bobby or not because his mother chose that moment to give his face a quick wipe round with a damp cloth and tell him to get a move on. Dressing didn't take long. His hair had been sheared off leaving only a short 'quiff' at the front which, if it wasn't elegant, didn't require much attention. By the time he was ready so was breakfast. There was a slice of bread and margarine on the table for each child to be washed down with a cup of watery tea. Joe ate quickly then sat looking at the two slices left for their dad. Jimmy munched his slice slowly, carefully looking anywhere but at his dad's bread.

His dad was drinking tea from a mug. His mam said the tea was so strong it would turn his insides brown. His dad just laughed and said, 'it sets me up for the day,' even a day like today when he had to go coal-gathering at Ryhope tip. It had been snowing overnight so maybe there wouldn't be as many people as usual, but you could never tell till you got there.

Whatever the day would bring, the minute brought a mug of

strong tea so hot Jimmy could have sworn it was still bubbling. It must have been good because, after a quick glance at the two boys, his dad pushed the slices of bread and marg towards them. Jimmy mumbled, 'Thanks Da,' but his dad just bent his head over his mug. Maybe he was staring down into the mug for warmth, Jimmy thought, watching tendrils of steam curl round his father's moustache. His dad sat there for a long time and, when he finally did look up, it was to turn to Jimmy's mother. He made an odd movement with his hands in front of his chest as if closing or fastening something. Though he didn't speak, she answered with a shake of the head.

Tea and breakfast over – dinner and supper too for that matter – his dad set off for Ryhope with a coal-sack under his arm. Oddly, he didn't put on his top coat though Jimmy knew Aunt Nellie had brought his dad one round after his uncle had died. When Jimmy grew up he was going to drink tea hot and strong. It must stop you feeling the cold. Meanwhile his mam told him strong tea was bad for young kidneys. He'd have to put up with the cold the same way all his friends had to.

When he and Joe set off for school, two of his friends shouted, 'Happy New Year.' There was little evidence yet of the newness of the year. The only arrival had been snow and even that couldn't decide whether to stay. Although it reached his ankles, it was soft and slushy underneath. The slush squidged up between his toes with every step. He didn't dawdle.

When they reached school, Jimmy and Joe made their way to stand under the red brick arches with the other barefoot children. They stayed there, where it was dry, watching the children with footwear playing in the yard. Bobby, of the new boots, was now neither fish nor fowl and hovered between the groups, worried the snow might damage his status symbols.

Jimmy shifted from foot to foot longing for bell-time. His teacher Miss Weston, a stout, middle-aged, kindly soul, would, he knew, let them gather round the meagre classroom fire. A few at a time, they'd huddle in a semicircle until they were warm or at least thawed at the edges. The small coal allowance meant the air beyond a twelve inch radius held little more than a hint of warmth but Jimmy still welcomed it.

The fire was the only bright spot in a dismal classroom decorated in middle-earth colours and Jimmy's attention was divided between fire and blackboard. On the blackboard, Miss Weston inscribed letters so perfectly formed that Jimmy was torn between despair and yearning admiration. Here was evidence it was possible to write any letter many times and have it look exactly the same each time. No allowances could be made, at least not openly, for hands that shook with cold, so Jimmy often felt disheartened.

Miss Weston was not easily discouraged. When the firelight attracted more than its share of glances, she paused in front of the class, creating an air of stillness about her that demanded attention.

'This,' she said, tapping the blackboard, 'What is this?'

'The way out, Miss Weston,' the class replied. It was the introductory joke for each new class, an initiation ceremony she carried out each September.

'Where is the way out children? Point to the way out.' Hands would point to the door and bodies would relax, relieved they knew the answer to the first question their new teacher asked.

'No. Wrong!' she'd say triumphantly and, guaranteed a good audience, would explain learning was the only way out.

Today Jimmy continued to stare at the fire. It had started snowing again and he was wondering if his dad would turn back or walk on to Ryhope. He didn't know which he hoped for. It sounded daft. If his dad had to buy coal there'd be less money for food but, for the last three months, the fire had been a double-edged sword for Jimmy.

However carefully you picked coal, you always got bits of stone or slate in with it. Each night Jimmy had to make a choice: get close and risk being burnt by a flying fragment of stone or stay back in the cold. The others jumped, then laughed whenever there was a sharp crack. Even if they were caught, they'd hop round the room shouting, then return to the fireside. Jimmy was different, he hated the noise and the way you could never anticipate the next crackshot. His dad understood having been in the trenches during the Great War, the last months of which he spent wondering not if, but when, he'd die. He laughed at nobody's fears. The rest of the family could, and did, laugh at Jimmy.

One night, when the fire was spluttering more than usual, dad told them he'd heard there was a carpenter's job going in New-castle. He was going there in the morning. If he was hired it would mean moving, but it was a Corporation Job, even worth moving to Newcastle for. He'd borrow Uncle Tom's suit, carry it with him, and an old army friend in Newcastle would let him wash and change at his house. You didn't go job hunting looking as if you'd walked fifteen miles, even if you had.

When his dad got out the mirror and started to trim his moustache, Jimmy moved near the fire. If he could stay there, without jumping the next three times the fire cracked, he knew his dad would get the job. He sat for ages, rigid with concentration. Two loud bangs, one straight after the other broke his concentration, and he jumped. A tiny flake of slate landed on his knee and stuck there. It hardly hurt at all really, but he cried as though heartbroken. He cried again when his dad got home and told them there hadn't been a vacancy. It had just been one of the many rumours that floated round. He would never know that, curled up on his father's lap, he had provided a cover for his father's tears. All he knew was that his father held him for a long time, till he slept. He woke to find his father drinking his hot, strong tea as usual. Jimmy cheered up then but, long after he'd forgotten about his plea-bargaining with Fate, his spirits would plummet whenever a fire spat stone or slate.

The classroom fire burned quietly, and Jimmy imagined he was toasting his feet inches away from the grate. Miss Weston saw, understood, but did not approve.

'James Smith! You ought to be burning to learn, not yearning to burn. What can you see in that fire boy? The future? A job? What do you want to be, boy?'

Jimmy was too wise to say the first thing that came into his head. Had he said, 'I want to be a boxer like Jack Casey, Miss,' retribution would have been swift. The only time Miss Weston had been known to lose her temper had been when, one year, she'd discovered that sixteen boys and four girls had wanted to be boxers.

'Dunno, Miss,' he mumbled.

'You'll know by tomorrow. Write two pages on "My chosen work".' It seemed short notice to decide the rest of his life but Jimmy believed Miss Weston would know if his commitment to his chosen work was anything less than total. The rest of the day hung round him like chains.

He went home from school with Billy. He liked Billy and Billy's mother even more. Billy was a rarity, an only child. His father had a good job as a Corporation Road Sweeper and his mother was kind. Jimmy often stood in front of their fire eating big jam sandwiches. The jam wasn't scraped on either, but spread, so it had been known to ooze out of the edges.

That afternoon Mrs Charlton said, 'I've got something for you,' and, taking a pair of boots from a cupboard, handed them to him. He just stood staring down at them. She pushed his arm, 'Go on then, try them on. They're too small for Billy. Him and his dad have feet like herring-boxes.'

Jimmy's hands shook as he fumbled with the thick leather but – joy of joys – they fitted. Not only that, but there was a good two inches' growing room. They were Jimmy's, if not for life, at least till he could no longer squeeze his feet into them. Jimmy tried curling up his toes and decided that would be a long time yet. As soon as he got home, he had to return to Mrs Charlton's with his mother to thank her properly.

'Now don't go on about it,' Mrs Charlton insisted, 'I've not forgotten your kindness with the meat.'

Later, when Jimmy asked about the meat, his ma yelled, 'Don't say nowt about any meat.' He didn't care about meat, he'd only asked out of devilment. Having boots gave you the heart for a bit of mischief.

He took one of the boots to bed and lay in the dark running his fingers along the rows of stitching. A man would have to be strong to pierce such thick leather with such neat stitches. As he went to sleep, he was thinking about the essay he'd written. 'Some day soon people will have enough money to buy boots. I'm going to be a cobbler and make them.'

Miss Weston read his essay in silence. Jimmy and Billy hovered round her desk, awaiting her reaction.

Finally she spoke, 'Everybody able to afford shoes!' she snorted. Her eyes widened as she saw Jimmy's feet were now encased in more than enough leather for his small feet but, without hesitating she turned on Billy, 'And you Billy Charlton. What do you want to be? An electrician? I suppose that you think that one day people will be able to afford electricity in their homes?'

Billy, bewildered by her harshness, whispered, 'No, Miss Weston.'

Jimmy wasn't so sure. If he could acquire a pair of boots, and find out what he was going to be when he grew up, all in one day, well then, anything was possible!

June Fairweather

■ A man like Mulloy ■

It was a humid July afternoon; Casey sat on a heap of bricks munching his sandwiches. He didn't seem to take much interest in his can of hot tea or the daily paper which lay at his feet. His thoughts for the moment were on other things – like Mulloy, for instance, who strutted casually up to the site. He always felt so cocksure of himself. If ever a man was a tower of strength, Mulloy was, both mentally and physically. Casey wished he could be like this, be 'the hard man' and not give a damn for anyone or anything.

Casey wasn't long on the job, or long in this country for that matter. The smell of the fresh-cut grass came drifting from an adjoining field and sent his thoughts winging westwards to Galway where his heart was. What was Kathleen up to now, he wondered. Haymaking, maybe, in the long meadow with her father, her auburn hair tumbling down her forehead, like the burnished autumn leaves tumble, topsy-turvy, from the trees in October. Her impish smile still taunted him, despite the fact, their parting was a turbulent affair.

'You don't have to go,' she scolded. 'There's plenty of work in Ireland now – not like in our father's day. It was different then! People had to go.'

'I know, I know,' he said, fumbling for words. 'It's only for a while, and it will give us time to think things over. Anyway, I love you, so what's the difference!'

They stood there, exchanging small talk. Then she kissed him hurriedly before he stepped on board the train. She walked briskly down the platform towards the exit, never even giving a backward glance or a wave of her hand.

He kept leaning out of the carriage window long after she had gone. What in the hell was he going for, he pondered. He knew she once had a crush on Andy Dolan and numerous times she had mentioned his name. Now she could have him if she wanted to.

Slumping back on the seat as the train pulled out, he half knew why he was going. It was a strange mixture of love and jealousy that was driving him away from Mulldara and from Kathleen. His head was in a whirl of jumbled thoughts as a voice called in the distance, not Jimmy, as he was used to, but, 'Casey', 'Casey'. It got louder and louder: 'CASEY', CASEY'.

He came to, his head still in a kind of whirl and with the smell of sweet grass still all around him. It was not the soft cushioned seat of the carriage that supported him but the hard edge of common building bricks which bit into his back. Above him stood the heaving bulk of Mulloy.

'CASEY! Is it dead or sleeping you are?' he barked.

Slowly, like the moon breaking through the clouds, it dawned on Casey where he was and for a moment he felt sick.

'Do you know what time it is?' growled Mulloy.

Casey looked at him through a haze. 'No, I don't. What time is it?' he asked.

'Time you were over there in the footing, levelling that bleddy concrete, that's what time it is.'

Nonchalantly, Casey eased himself off the heap of bricks, picked up his can and paper and ambled over to where his mates were already working. Come Christmas he would pack the lousy job in anyway, he mused. Even though he had a sneaking admiration for Mulloy, there was something about him he just couldn't fathom. Somehow he was a man who was hard to get close to. He didn't mix easily and he had few friends.

Casey had learned from his mates that Mulloy had lived most of his life in England, coming over while still in his teens. He was married with a grown-up son and daughter. He was, too, a man who demanded his pound of flesh, and men were sent packing if they failed to put in what he felt was a fair day's work. But those who pulled their weight got top wages and Mulloy saw to that.

As time went by, Casey proved that he could hold his own with the best of them. He was conscious of his slight build, so deep down he had the idea that he had to prove to Mulloy that he was a tower of strength, 'a hard man', who didn't give a damn for anyone, including Mulloy himself.

For a while now Casey had been at loggerheads with the world; the reason being of course that no letter had been forthcoming from Kathleen Kelly since the day he'd left.

That Tuesday morning when Casey clocked in, Mulloy was waiting for him. 'We work here on Mondays too, Casey,' he said soberly.

'So what.' Casey barked back at him. 'No work, no pay. Who's complaining?'

Mulloy took a few deliberate strides in Casey's direction. 'I am,' he said, his face flushed from the insolence of his countryman.

'The job's got to be completed by the end of the month and it won't be done if we spend our time in The Heart and Hand, will it?'

'Call yourself an Irishman,' said Casey with a snarl. 'Do you know what day it was yesterday?'

'Monday,' said Mulloy grimacing, 'and you weren't at work.'

'A fella that can't afford to take St. Patrick's Day off isn't worth calling an Irishman,' said Casey adamantly, punching his card in the time clock with vengeance.

There was a frozen stare on Mulloy's countenance. This little upstart was beginning to bug him. He placed his hand on Casey's shoulder and swung him around with the ease that the wind turns a weather vane.

'Look here, you Spalpian,' balled Mulloy vehemently. 'I've spent more St. Patrick Days in the boozer than you have years on your shoulders, but I wised-up, and you will too, if you have any grey matter in that thick skull of yours.'

Casey shrugged past him, a leering scowl on his face. 'If only he had size on his side he would have 'planted one' on Mulloy at that minute, but Mulloy's towering frame reminded him that discretion was the better part of valour. He went down the site, his head throbbing from a terrible hangover. But more than that, his heart was throbbing with disappointment. Kathleen hadn't even bothered to send him a spray of shamrock. Bitterness was biting into him. Yesterday, he'd got up early and waited for the postman, but he had passed by as if Casey did not exist. He spent the day and his money drowning his sorrows along with drowning the shamrock that he never received.

Mulloy stood at a distance and marvelled at Casey's vitality, but deep down this fellow puzzled him. He was aloof and insolent but he wasn't work-shy; he'd give him that much.

That Thursday when Casey received his wages he stared wide-eyed at his pay-packet. This man Mulloy was a mystery. One day he railroads him for having a day off, the next day he gets paid in full as if nothing ever happened. What in the hell was he up to, anyway? For two pins he'd throw it in his face.

No, he didn't want to trade words with Mulloy, he reflected. He felt there was a soft centre somewhere under that hard crust but he would never get close enough to know. Soon the job would be finished; their ways would diverge, and that would be that.

Autumn was in the air now and the melancholy which that season always seems to bring somehow had rubbed off on Casey. He was in a thoughtful mood. His thoughts were drifting more and more towards Mulldara. And Kathleen Kelly. The urge to return home nagged him with each passing day. The job was almost at an end and it was as good an excuse as any for going back. Kathleen would not come to him. One thing the parting had done was to purge him of his pride, and jealousy. Inwardly he was homesick. He could never have done what Mulloy had done: spend his years away from Ireland and those he held dear.

It was during the last week on the site that the barrier between the two men partially came down.

'You're leaving us, then,' said Mulloy, his voice dropping to a whisper as he handed Casey his wages.

'Yes, I – I – I am,' stammered Casey.

'You don't like it here?' enquired Mulloy.

'Oh, I do, I do,' replied Casey readily, 'but I like the old Dart better.'

'It's hard leaving home,' said Mulloy thoughtfully. 'But it's harder leaving those you love.'

For a moment Casey thought Mulloy was endowed with the gift of extrasensory perception and could see into his affairs. It was only later that he learned the real meaning of Mulloy's words. After five years' absence Mulloy had decided that he would live out the remainder of his days in Ireland. His family were grown up and could look after themselves. It was time to retire, and the 'Old Country' was calling him back. But love was a powerful thing; whenever he thought of his children he knew what real love meant. They made no demands on him not to return. They remembered from their youth his dream: to live out his retirement years in Ireland. Now they would not stand in his way.

As Casey left the site on that final day, he was a changed man. He was not so wrapped up in himself as when he had first arrived and somehow he felt that, like this man Mulloy, he too was beginning to realise that true love makes no demands. Kathleen, by her silence, made none on him.

Michael Hannon

■ A change of heart ■

'Evening Star Classified, can I help you?' said a bright cheerful voice. Anne put her hand up to move her headphones, straightening the mouthpiece which by this time had drooped a little.

'We sell cars, houses and jobs. Anything that desires a market, we provide it,' said Liz Hooke, Executive Advertising Supervisor, as she stood behind a wooden stand which housed her notes. She spoke to the trainees like a priest from a pulpit. The logic was simple.

'The more space they purchase, the more likely it is that their advert will be seen by the potential buyers, so the more likely that they'll sell their houses or cars or whatever.' She smiled a glowing smile and Anne wondered whether she was going to say, 'Amen'.

Anne had found this advertising business quite exciting after three years of working in the securities department of an established merchant bank. Well, that had been at first. Everybody was so nice. She had been really taken aback by the way that they were all on first name terms with each other. This had seemed progressive. She had managed to call Liz Hooke 'Liz' after only one morning. That was unusual for Anne because normally it took her much longer than that to get to know people. There seemed to be none of those divisions between men and women that she had experienced in the bank. Liz had stated quite clearly that, 'In advertising, sex is not important.'

The trainees had tittered at this but then Liz always was a bit of a joker. After they had stopped, she had donated a wide toothy smile to proceedings and went on, 'Success in this job depends on how well or badly we serve the customer. We are only here to help them. Advertising provides a vital service which could not be found anywhere else.' This had been Liz's finishing statement and it concluded a week of theorizing on the art of advertising. Anne went home to her husband and said, 'At last, I've found a worthwhile job.'

The following Monday Anne was put into a pool where she was to begin her job. It took her until break on Wednesday afternoon to realise that all was not as it seemed.

The 'pool' was a large office not particularly noted for its interior design. It housed numerous rows of desks and at the top end of the room on a platform sat Liz. The place had the air of a Victorian schoolroom.

The 'boys and girls', as they were called, sat in these rows, attached to their desks by the wires of their headphones and waited for incoming phone calls.

Anne was sitting in the third row and spent her day facing the back of the person in front. The only person whose eyes she ever met was Liz who every now and then turned on an encouraging smile and then went immediately back to studying her nails.

The calls came thick and fast and Anne was tutored by a superior into expanding the desires of the client from two-line adverts into inch or half inch boxes with a heading in heavy, black type.

'Who'll notice two-line ads?' Liz would often ask. Another trainee, George who remarked that his uncle often scoured the small ads for bargains, was immediately frozen by a look from Liz. She smiled before she delivered her argument,

'Yes, but there aren't many like him, are there George?' George only lasted a few weeks. 'He couldn't cope,' Liz said at the weekly pep talk.

Business was good, and commission was a topic which was discussed in every spare moment. There were those who always did well and so treated the subject as an irrelevancy. Those who did badly also viewed the subject from this angle, although from different motives. The main bulk of the operators were those who bordered from average to good. It was these people who jealously counted up each line gained and translated it into pennies and pounds. Anne had fitted somewhere within this group.

When she had first realised that her job did not involve her being a kind of consumer welfare worker, she had made excuses,

'Well, people have to have somewhere to advertise, don't they? And they need professional people to help advise them.' A few weeks later she was heard to say, 'They make money selling their cars and houses, don't they? Why shouldn't we make some too?' And a month or so later,

'It's just a job. I might as well make as much as I can while I'm here.

It was about a week after this that Anne had decided to try and break her record commission level. It was Thursday afternoon and she was slightly ahead of her target for the day. It was five twenty-five and she decided to make the next call her last before going home. 'Make it a detached house in Barnet,' she thought. That was an inch and a half block or maybe even a mini display. In fact the voice of an old woman came over her earphones. She sounded a little distant and Anne said in her nicest voice, 'Could you speak up a little, dear?' The old woman was mumbling something about a lost pet and Anne felt a sense of impatience. It was five thirty and she wanted to get home. A lost pet ad wasn't worth a light.

'Look dear, can you speak a little more slowly,' she said in a harsher voice. No point in putting on the niceties, Anne thought, this is definitely a two-liner. The old woman began again, and Anne began to copy down the details. She contemplated cutting her off. Then she could go home. The two-line advert would only cut down her overall average. She looked up at Liz who was sitting in her usual position and who, it had been rumoured, had a tiny earphone which meant that she could cut into any call at any time. She couldn't risk cutting the old dear off. Her mind went back to the call and she instantly realised that the old woman was crying. Her cat had disappeared the day before yesterday. Did she think it could have got run over, or taken away? What did she think? Anne was stumped by this. This wasn't in the script. How the hell should she know whether it had got run over or not? Her anger turned to pity and she tried to draw the old woman around. She stopped crying, and Anne began to word the advert. She felt touchy and the back of her throat felt tight and sore. She read the price of the advert over to the woman.

'Oh, I couldn't afford that, dear,' said the old woman in a crackly voice. After a moment or two's hesitation she rang off. 'What a waste of time,' Anne thought. Surely the old girl knew the price of adverts? She totalled up her lines for the day and went off home. She felt annoyed. Her depression increased on the train and she spent the evening in a bad mood.

The next day was slow, and it was obvious to Anne that she would not break her commission level. She thought about the cat. And the old lady. She was hot and tired and went to the ladies room. She found herself crying. 'She would have been better ringing the local paper anyway,' Anne thought. 'It's not my problem. It's not my job to find her cat.'

Liz was horrified to find one of her very favourite op.s in this emotional state and immediately sent her home with a packet of panadol and a sympathetic expression.

Anne stayed for another few weeks and then handed in her notice. When Liz asked her why, she said,

'I just don't know. I can't put my finger on it.'

Anne Gebbett

■ Nothing surprised me at Grumpton's ■

Nothing surprised me at Grumpton's. I knew he would send for me, and that morning he did. It was Hazel who brought me the message in the foundry as I checked some castings ready for dispatch.

As I walked down the long passage towards his office, I noticed that the linoleum had broken and lifted outside the canteen, causing a safety hazard. That would have to be mended, I thought, before the safety officer spotted it. I mentioned it to old Sid Bramble, the odd-job man and toilet attendant who was leaning on a sweeping brush, reading the racing page.

I climbed the threadbare carpet on the stairs, stepping out on the landing on to new Wilton which spread underneath the door of Grumpton's office. I thought how odd it was that as his office was approached the floor covering grew more luxurious. Knocking on the door, I thought of that day, more years ago than I wanted to remember, when I first walked that way through Grumpton's. Same lino, different carpet.

I heard Grumpton growling at me to enter, and as I did so he invited me to sit down in the vacant chair he always kept the other side of his desk. I knew his opening words,

'How long have you been with us now?'

I restrained a strong impulse to say, 'Too bloody long,' and instead replied, 'Since leaving the navy, Mr Grumpton.' After all these years I still called him 'Mr Grumpton'.

'Well,' he answered, 'You know why I've called you in here.' I knew all right.

He went on, 'Bob's job has now become vacant and the management committee has voted you the best man to fill it.'

Lying bastard. There was no voting on the management committee. Grumpton spoke, they listened. Then he looked straight at me and said, 'Think you can handle it?'

I stifled a yawn. I'd been helping Bob with the job for nearly two years. We practically did it together as a double act.

Bob started two weeks before me which gave him seniority (such things counted for a lot at Grumpton's) and when the bottle killed old man Dawson, Bob took over the job, and all the blame that went with it.

Now Bob was dead. Heart attack over his desk with what should have been another good forty years in front of him; and I was being offered his job.

'Yes, I think I can handle it Mr Grumpton,' I found myself saying, trying to sound enthusiastic.

'Good,' he said. 'As from right now, start moving into your office. Get Sid or someone to help you.' He then smiled that sickly smile I had grown over the years to hate. 'You're on my management committee now,' he said. 'I'll get a memo put out about it to all employees right now.'

We shook hands, and I started to walk out of the office. As I reached the door, I heard Grumpton call me. I looked around and saw him standing over his desk as if about to make an after dinner speech. He cleared his throat, 'You understand,' he said, 'I expect results or there may have to be,' his voice dropped, 'changes.'

I knew what he meant by changes and I nodded slowly. As I walked down to Bob's office, Sid Bramble was mending the lino. When he saw me he grinned and waved wildly at me pointing proudly to what he had done. Sid was one of the most popular employees at Grumpton's. The story was that years ago, before the days of reasonable industrial compensation, he was badly burnt when the iron furnace exploded due to company neglect. The case was hushed up and settled out of court, and Sid came out of it with a contract to work at Grumpton's for life; plus scrambled brains to go with it.

Everyone knew that Grumpton would have sacked Sid years

ago if he could, but to do so would have cost him thousands.

We all liked Sid who enjoyed nothing better than bragging how many years he'd worked at the place, though most of his work consisted of snoozing the day away in the toilets. He knew how to keep the place clean and he knew that whatever he did he couldn't be sacked, but he didn't know much else.

I walked through the door of Bob's office and remembered the last time I had seen him in that room. He was slumped forwards over the desk, head sideways, eyes open. Then I remembered Julie's tearfully bitter words at the funeral with Charles' arm around her, 'That bloody job killed my husband.' Strange how her attitude had changed. After Bob's promotion, she had organised a party inviting everyone to it: now she was the grieving widow. But Julie would be all right. Bob's life assurance policies and Charles Beckford would see to that. I wondered if Bob knew about Julie and Charles . . . But who can tell what a dead man knew?

I decided to confirm the news that evening to Stella. I knew that I would feel like a drink and a chat about it by then, but definitely no party. The kids might get their bikes for Christmas after all, I thought.

But one thing I was already sure of. The bloody job was not going to give me a heart attack or put me on the bottle like it did old man Dawson.

I told Bob once it was two men's work. 'Three,' he said, 'If you include Grumpton, who spends more time walking across golf courses than he does walking through his own foundry.'

I wondered how my position in management would affect my work in the union. I would obviously be expected to resign. When I started at Grumpton's no union existed. Then out of necessity one was born, with no small thanks to Bob and myself. Over the years it had grown stronger, not without good cause, giving Grumpton more than one headache. It had already occurred to me that perhaps that was why Grumpton offered me the job as the union would in no way allow a manager to participate in its affairs.

Suddenly I had an overwhelming desire to walk back up to Grumpton's office and tell him to stick his job. But I didn't. I wish I had now. Anyway, it was too late. I saw Grumpton from the window start up his car and drive away; no doubt exhausted after another day's hard graft getting that memo put out to all employees, and it wasn't even eleven o'clock.

That was it. I took the job and started wearing my suit to

work. I even discarded the supermarket bag in which I used to bring my sandwiches, using instead a leather briefcase, as all proper managers do; except mine was plastic. I even had allocated to me a parking space for a car I didn't possess.

I stood the traditional round of lunchtime drinks at the Royal George, where, if Sid Bramble had had his way, I would have stood them all the rest of the week and for ever more. But, at last, I knew I'd made the big time. I knew then that all the studying I'd done at night school so long ago had not been in vain.

It didn't make any difference. After a few months, I received my redundancy notice through the post along with everyone else. (Grumpton had sold his foundry to a big building-company who wanted the land it stood on for a multi-storey car park.) I received a month's notice in accordance with my contract; some only had a week.

Sid Bramble couldn't understand the prospect of being unemployed. Even with all the money Grumpton was obliged to pay him. God knows, it wasn't for the want of explaining it to him. And he did tell us he understood. I personally told him that when he collected his cash it would then be his turn to stand the lunchtime drinks in the Royal George. He laughed and waved in his usual cheery way telling me he would. But he never collected his cash. On that last day he walked across the yard to his beloved lavatories. He sat down and scribbled out a few illegible words on some toilet paper, then he unwrapped a shotgun he had managed to smuggle into work hidden in a blanket. He placed it under his chin and fired both barrels.

I had to inform the police, and clean up the mess. But nothing surprised me at Grumpton's.

Terry Lee

■ The water rats ■

There was unrest among the men. For days it had been in the air. They walked the roadways of darkness, a chain of figures lit up by the soft glare of their lamps. On their tired, pale faces, turned towards the rail track on which they walked, was an irritable expression.

It was quite a step from pit-bottom to the coalface and the silent, dark, rock-cold roads turned and twisted like paths in a wood. The hard ground between the rails echoed their footsteps rhythmically, like the beating of drums. They moved along the roads silently, thinking hard, and it seemed that their anger was being questioned by the darkness.

They were a ragged lot of men, turned and weathered by the pit's ways and dangers. They varied in stature. Some were tall and thin, others short and sturdy, but all of them were strong, durable and tough with courage indelibly stamped in blue accident-marks on their rock-pinched hands and torsos.

In the chain of men walked Jo Morgan, a man of medium height with powerful shoulders and hands and a determined, lined face.

Suddenly the silence was disturbed by a man's voice as though at that particular moment, and at all costs, he must express himself. Others joined in until the road was filled with angry, involved voices. Then the voice of Jo Morgan rose above them like an explosion,

'Shut up, all of you, shut up!'

The voices toned down, and once again there was silence. Putting their hand-lamps to the ground, they prepared themselves to listen.

The speaker stared through the semidarkness into their angry faces.

'Look what comes of talking,' he began. 'The manager talks, the under-manager talks, the district official talks, everybody talks and nothing happens. What do they think we are, water rats? We're all right now, but water can rot you, as fast as dust. We've got to get that allowance. We can't earn any extra . . .'

The speaker's face had grown wild. His eyes revealed a man who was seeking revenge, revenge against officials and conditions of water which crippled a man.

The others digested his words and were further angered. They were breathing anger. It was rushing in their blood, tingling in their nerves, churning up their memories of other old grievances.

'We'll strike!' shouted a man.

'I'm with you!' shouted another.

'Who the hell do they think they are!' shouted a third. 'Let's turn back now!'

The rest were excited, inspired to action and deeply involved in the sting of words, words of revenge, meaningful and inspiring words. Almost in a chorus they shouted, 'Let's get out, now!'

'No!' shouted Jo Morgan, cutting in. 'Listen, listen carefully. We'll try once again. If we get the same cold shoulders, we'll come out . . . understand?'

He said the words slowly, stabbing them between his teeth and using his hands.

They muttered approval. The force of Jo Morgan's words and hands held them to understanding. They picked up their lamps and started to move on again, changing from one hand to the other, for the lamps were heavy. They had taken one small step towards a reconciliation of their problem.

They continued their journey and turned over in their minds what they were going to say and how they would say it. Wasn't Seth Thomas finished by water? Weren't his hands useless, as stiff as signal wire? Wasn't his chest bronchial? That was water, and Seth without compensation . . . What was the way to the truth? Water had a way of ruining you, cunningly, without it showing much . . .

Presently they came to a junction of roads and they took a sharp turning to the left, which brought them into a road known as the Straight Deep. At the bottom of the Deep was a lamp station built into the side of the road. Inside, the district official waited. He sat on an old, wooden box, resting his back and head against a seam of coal sandwiched between two layers of silica rock. His face and eyes were motionless. He was thinking hard and staring into the roadway outside. Near him on the wooden box lay his helmet. Attached to a nail on a crooked, vertical post in one corner was his lamp, lighting up dully a jagged wall and a patch of the roadway outside, like a light falling from a curtained window. His hair, brown and dusty, dropped over his forehead. He appeared to be on the verge of sleep; his eyes opened, then closed for several seconds. Now and again he pulled himself from his back rest and listened, turning an ear towards the door frame. Eventually he got up and roused himself in a weary, careful fashion. He moved to the entrance and stood against the wooden framework of the doorway and gazed sleepily into the darkness of the main road. A deep silence surrounded the lamp station, broken only occasionally by the shuffle of rats. Far away in the road appeared tiny lights, accompanied by the muffled sound of footsteps. The footsteps grew louder and the lights brighter.

When the men arrived at the lamp station, they gathered around the doorway. The official, cold and unfriendly, gave each lamp a twist at the bottom to check that it was locked. After all the lamps had been checked Jo Morgan spoke, 'What time will you be around this morning?'

'Can't say. I've got a lot to do first. Any time after eleven I should say.'

The men continued their journey towards the coalface. The official returned to his seat in the station. He began again to think and stare into the roadway and to close his eyes. He was puzzled by Jo Morgan's question. The men had arrived later than usual. He had sensed something odd and virile in the faces of the men. He sat up, took a sandwich from his jacket pocket and began eating. Two mice crept out of a dark corner and ran along the bottom edge of the box to where the official's feet dangled upon the crumbs dropped from the sandwich. The official spotted them and crunched the remains of the sandwich in his fist, showering the mice with crumbs. He lifted his legs up on to the box and lay in a horizontal position, watching with childlike curiosity the hungry mice feeding below. Other mice joined the party. Some came from the dark roadway, sniffing the air with their pointed noses.

When the men reached the coalface they undressed, unlocked their tools and took up positions along the face. The seam of coal was six feet thick and stretched a distance of a hundred yards. Parallel to the coalface was a rail track on which rested a line of empty trams waiting to be filled. From the floor a spring of water bubbled, collecting in pools along the uneven surface. Water trickled from the roof between vertical posts. The posts, standing close together, resembled a wood of pine trees.

The sound of mandrills, heavy hammers and crunching coal resounded along the face. Lamps hung from the posts, shining dreary light on the men moving in a rhythm of work. Not many minutes passed before water kissed the hot steaming bodies, soaked the scanty vests and ran down trouser legs, sticking to wet, muscle-tense skin. The floor water filled boots and mirrored the lamp lights, like a wet street at night.

Later that morning the official began his rounds of inspection, walking along the coalface and studying the wet, treacherous roof. As he passed each man they spoke to him, debating the conditions and making a claim for an allowance. In a nonchalant way, the official replied to each man, using the same words:

'Impossible, my hands are tied in such matters. The water won't last long. It'll probably be gone in a week or two.'

His attitude provoked them. Jo Morgan, fixing a post some

distance away, left his work and faced the official, hitching up his wet trousers and wiping the water from his hair and face before he spoke.

'You'll know well enough we should get an allowance for this lot!' began Jo emphatically. 'Are you trying to run the district on the cheap? Do you get a bonus for keeping the cost down?'

The men left their sections of the face and gathered to listen.

'Look, Jo,' said the official, 'this pit is on its last legs. Things are tight now . . .'

'And we'll be on our last legs if we stay too long in this rain. What do you think we are, water rats? We don't count I suppose – keep the cost down and never mind the water rats. At least give us something extra for rheumatics. No allowance, no more work. We're going out . . . now!'

The men backed him.

'Yes, out,' they muttered.

The official retreated in a vicious mood, cursing the men under his breath as he went. He got to the main road and stepped inside a recess where a telephone hung.

The telephone rang in the cabin at the pit-bottom, where the manager was sitting. He rose to his feet to answer it. He listened and nodded his head as the district official explained carefully.

'Who's their spokesman?' he asked.

'Jo Morgan, boss.'

'When are they leaving the face?'

'Anytime now, boss.'

'Talk to them again at the lamp station. Try and get them to finish the shift. We've got to keep that face open, understand. We can't let water get the upper hand or it'll be a write off.'

'Right, boss.'

The manager, a tall, lean man in his fifties, looked solemn and weary. But he was tough and fearless. The situation in the wet face irritated him. He had learnt to shed compassion during his many years as a mining official and to insulate himself from the physical hardships of men who worked in constant danger, semidarkness and water. That was why he was an efficient manager, a towering authority who made his petty officials jump at his command. He had told his officials, 'Give them twice the amount of work to do and half the pay, then you'll get your whack.'

He thought in terms of coal, yardage and labour machines of work.

He didn't want to see the men yet. He was the last resort, the last unbreakable fence to try and shatter. He felt amused and pompous at the thought of the interview. He knew the right words to cut across their argument, how to minimise their efforts, how to be hard, how to retract and heap on compliments, how to play one man against another with the promise of a place in a better part of the pit or a bit of extra overtime. He had many tricks up his pit-sleeve and he knew he could play his part. But it was too early yet for the final scene. He had the patience to wait, for waiting deliberately in the wings was an essential part of the drama.

The district official arrived at the lamp station, hung his lamp on one of the door posts and took off his helmet. He wiped the sweat from his forehead and eyes and bit off a chunk of plug tobacco, which he uncurled from his waistcoat pocket. He was sweating after his swift journey from the telephone recess about half a mile inside. He took off his jacket and flung it on the wooden box inside.

'As if I haven't enough problems!' he cried out in anguish.

In the distance, footsteps padded softly on the hard ground. The official stared along the dark road. He spotted a cluster of lights in the distance.

'Bloody fools!' he muttered.

He stood in the middle of the road and wiped his coarse hand over his troubled face. He looked at the roof and at the oncoming men. First he stood on one foot and then on the other, muttering threats under his breath, like a soldier waiting for the enemy to approach before firing. He began to feel a little afraid, chewing his plug tobacco in little, quick bites, moving his lips like a rabbit. After all, he thought, the conditions were bad. He'd never seen the like of it before. You couldn't blame them. That water could ruin a man's health, stiffen him up and finish him for work.

The lights got bigger and brighter. He began to think of the manager's words:

'Try and get them to finish the shift. We've got to keep that face open.'

He began to rehearse what he would say to the men when they arrived. He mumbled words, gesticulated with his hands and raised his eyebrows. His nerves were at breaking point. He felt trapped between the men and the manager, who would be waiting for him up at the Officials' Lodge on the surface.

Soon the men came within sight out of the darkness, angry, wet, determined. When they were at arms length the official spoke,

'Where are you lot going then?'

87

He faced them, pushing his thumbs behind his belt. They gathered around him, the stains of pit-water dry in streaks upon their disturbed faces. Dozens of stinging eyes gazed at him. He stepped across the rails, retreating from their fierce expressions.

'We're going out,' growled Jo Morgan. 'You know why. We don't have to go over it all again.'

'Look, why don't you all go back and think it over. Finish the shift first, and then we'll talk it over. The water won't be there forever. The manager said it would be gone in a fortnight or so.'

'A fortnight!' said Jo. 'It's been there eight weeks now and it's getting worse, not better. We'll all be stiff men before its gone. Who's going to pay us for rheumatics? Come on lads, let's get out of these holes.'

They brushed the official to one side and walked briskly away feeling exhilarated and courageous for what they were doing. But they were still agitated and now and then a man would burst out with a threat or repeat something that had already been said.

On they went along the dark roads. Their lights shone upon their crouched, drying bodies and upon the floor in shivering patches. They were going out, going home, away from the cold, killing water. They were making a stand.

'We'll show them!' called out an angry voice as the men poured out of the cage at the pit-surface.

'We'll do the same again if we don't get any allowance!' shouted another.

The men chuckled approval. It was the last shift of the week and they had an extra interest in the daylight which blazed into their squinting eyes.

Monday morning was cold and dark. Snow fell on the buildings and machines, changing the shapes into copies of marble sculpture. The ground was clothed in a white carpet patterned with footprints. From the lamp room to the pit-gear, men drifted over the snow quietly, their greatcoats patched with snow. Swinging lamps lit up the tumbling snowflakes. At the pit-gear men stood chatting and stamping their feet to keep them warm.

'Have you 'eard,' said one man to another as they stepped into a cage, 'the manager's closed down the wet seam?'

'Aye,' said the other, 'and the water rats are redundant.'

'Pity,' said the first man, 'and so near Christmas too.'

The gate clicked as it locked and the cage disappeared into the dark shaft.

Robert Morgan

■ Victorian piece ■

I stood perfectly still just behind the closed kitchen door waiting for my father to speak. He sat before a flickering fire in a high-back, wooden chair, his chair; nobody else was allowed to sit in it, except occasionally my mother did, when he wasn't there. One of his hobnailed boots rested on the fender; his legs were still tied beneath the knees to keep the rats at work from running up his legs. He was bent forward, one arm on his raised knee, sucking at his empty clay pipe, gazing into the flames. I knew he was choosing his words carefully for the time when he would speak to me. The slow ticking of the clock and the soft glow from the oil lamp on the table made everything seem normal for my weekly meeting with my father. But I was uneasy, almost frightened; events were taking place that I had no control over. I was wearing boots, black, woollen stockings, my best knee breeches, a clean, well-darned shirt and a jacket. What made this unusual was that I'd also had a bath, and it wasn't even Friday. I hardly ever wore boots and had never had stockings before. My mother stood behind me, her red, sore hands gripping my shoulders pulling me tight against her long, black dress. I could feel her bulge in my back that meant I was to have another brother or sister. Maybe. Her fingers hurt me, but never had I felt her love flow into me with, such intensity. I wanted to turn and comfort her, but she kept me facing my father.

He leant back in his chair; he was ready to speak. I watched his hands, but they didn't undo his belt. I sighed with relief; I wasn't expecting a beating but I could never be sure. Without looking up, he spoke: 'Come here boy.'

My mother gently patted my shoulders and pushed me towards my father. I heard a stiffled sob, and the door open and close behind me as I rounded the table and stood in front of my father.

'How old are you now lad?'

'I'm twelve and a quarter now, pappa.'

'A bit too old to still be sleeping with your sister, eh?'

'Yes, pappa.'

'But there is no room for you anywhere else is there?'

'No, pappa.'

'I've done all I can for you lad. I've got eight children now, and soon I'll have nine, and there's just not room for everybody, so something's gotta be done.'

'Yes, pappa.'

'As you're the eldest it falls on you, do you see that lad?'

'Yes, pappa.'

'You're not a lad any longer. Why, you're almost a man, and it's time for you to do a man's work.'

'Yes, pappa. May I speak?' He nodded. 'Where will I go? What will I do?'

'I've taken care of that for you, my son. You come with me tonight to accept the Queen's shilling.'

'What is that, pappa?'

'You're going to be a dummer in the Queen's Army, lad. That's. what that means. You're gonna be a soldier.'

Now I understood. I was leaving home because my father could no longer support me as well as all the others. He had done his best; he had found me a position where I would be looked after instead of throwing me out to fend for myself.

'Thank you, father. I'll not disgrace you.'

'I know that, son. Come, it's time we were off. Say goodbye to your mother, brothers and sisters. Oh, and promise your mother you'll get a message to her every now and then, so we know you are well.'

We walked towards the gas lamp at the end of our alley, my father making me keep close to the houses so that I wouldn't step into any puddles or muck that covered the cobblestones. As we approached the archway leading to the street, the yellow light from the gas lamp made it easier to see where I was going. We turned right on leaving the alleyway, and our boots crunched on paving stones. A fog was drifting up from the river, and as we got closer, it became thicker. We could hear the weary tread of a plodding horse pulling its cart, and from out of the gloom came a very tired man scuffling along leading the poor animal. The man wore a sack on his head with one corner inside the other, and so did the horse. Both trudged by with heads down, the horse and man taking the empty coal cart back to the yard. The man was either too tired to climb up on the shafts and stay there or he realised he needed his horse for tomorrow for another long, hard day. We walked towards yellow tents of light, through them, and into the grey fog beyond until we approached another gas lamp, and so it would begin again. Each deep in our own thoughts, neither of us spoke until we reached the Admiral Benbow.

'In here lad,' my father said and led me to a room off the public bar.

Inside, at a table, with a pint pot in front of him, was a soldier. He stood up as we entered. I gazed in awe at him, never had I seen such a fine sight of a man before: his boots were black and shiny, and he wore black trousers and a marvellous, scarlet tunic complete with a white belt and crosspiece, shiny, brass buttons, stripes on his arms and colourful medals on his chest. His face was tanned and healthy, and he had a fine bushy moustache, clear blue eyes, and on his head was a white helmet with a brass badge and spike. He stood upright as if on parade.

I looked at my father and noticed for the first time how stooped and pale he was, and a flood of deep sorrow passed through me.

'So this is the lad yer were telling me about Mr Atkins.'

'That's right, sergeant, and a good lad he is too.' The sergeant seated himself at the table, took off his helmet and placed it at the far end, opened a drawer and removed an ink well, a quill, a sheet of paper and a leather purse, these he placed in front of him. 'Well lad, so yer want the Queen's shilling, that's good 'cos we'll make a man of yer, we'll put food in yer belly, clothes on yer back, and give yer a fair measure of excitement. You'll 'ave plenty o' mates an' grow big an' strong. Why yer might become a general or even a sergeant like me. And not only that, we pays yer for the privilege of letting us do all that for yer. A nice drum for yer to bang about on all the time and a farthing a day for yerself to boot. What more could yer ask for lad, eh? Tell me that, what more could yer ask for?'

'Nothing sir.'

'Right, that's settled then, put yer mark here where me finger is.' He stabbed at the paper in front of him, then dipped the quill in the ink and handed it to me.

'Sergeant, my son can write his name and read.'

'Can 'e now, can 'e. Why, I do declare we've got hofficer material 'ere, that's what you are lad, hofficer material.'

I could see my father's eyes glow with pride. I bent my head and signed 'Tommy Atkins' with a flourish. I looked up at my father who seemed to have grown six inches during the past minute. The sergeant dipped into the small leather purse and handed me the Queen's shilling. I stared at it in the palm of my hand, the gas light making it shine and glitter, the first shilling I ever had, the first piece of silver I ever owned. I closed my fist and shook it just to feel the weight. It felt good. I opened my fist and asked the sergeant if he could change the coin. He did. I slipped sixpence down inside my stockings, the other I placed in my father's hand.

'For you, father, for you and mother.' He turned away and rubbed the back of his hand across his mouth and nose.

'Yer brought me a fine young man 'ere Mr Atkins who 'as proper respect for 'is parents.'

'Aye, I have that, sergeant. Tell me, for the sake of his mother, what happens to the lad now? Where will he go? She's bound to ask.'

'When we leaves 'ere, I'll take 'im to the barracks, there 'e'll get supper, bread an' sausage an' cocoa. After 'e goes to sleep in a bed of 'is own. In the morning, 'e 'as a wash an gets breakfast, after that we kits 'im out, uniform an' all. 'E'll get a drum, an' we teaches 'im the drills. At the end of the month we takes a nice sea voyage. A quick march down to the docks, board ship, sail down the river, why 'e'll even see the Rock of Gibralta an' the Mediterranean Sea'. The sergeant turned to me. 'Well boy, 'ow does it sound? Can yer see it? There'll be you, smart as a new pin out in front, beating, waving an' all. Can yer see it? I tell yer boy, yer gonna 'ave the time of yer life in the Crimea.'

Ron Wessex

■ Jimmy takes the lead ■

He was a burglar, like his dad and his dad's dad and his dad's dad's dad and *his* dad as well, for that matter.

'That,' said Jimmy to me one fine summer's morning, 'is what's called tradition!' Then he stared at me with his peculiar, daft-looking eyes, not sure whether to pat or pan me. Friendship with Jimmy was, to say the least, a balancing act. It struck me how little he talked: he said nothing yet got his own way. All the time they said he was thick, but they never caught him, did they?

I put it down to his attitude. He had this firm belief that he was not put on this earth to do as he was told. He was Jimmy and it was no good treating him like he was some bogger else. The world he saw was Jimmy's world; the other folk were there just so's he din't get lonely. It was funny the way they tried to tell him what to do in *his* world. Too funny to laugh at really.

When he was a kid, this certainty that he was the centre of the universe, led him to the natural conclusion that he was indestruct-able. Barry Protheroe jokingly dared him to jump off the railway bridge on Western Boulevard for a ha'penny. Jimmy promptly agreed and a little band of urchins followed him up the hill to make sure he didn't turn yickney. I was in our back garden at the time – having heard the racket – and was looking up at the bridge. I saw Jimmy hand his coat to one of the lads and hoist himself over the palings.

Somebody had to run to fetch his sister, and I remember her shouting, 'Jimmy don't, Jimmy don't!', as she ran along the lines towards him. At that exact moment, he released his grip and dropped slowly and gracefully to the tracks below. When he landed a cloud of dust arose, and through it I saw his left leg bending the wrong way as he hit the deck. A mighty scream rent the air: Jimmy was yelling from surprise and anger rather than pain. After that experience, he altered his philosophy slightly.

As soon as spotty puberty arrived, Jimmy enlarged. His chest filled out and his arms and neck became one. He walked in that unusual, weight-lifters' fashion, rolling ape-like from side to side. His arms, padded with over-developed muscles, stuck out at the front of his body, and his hands dangled at the ends so that he was forced to clench his fists, in case anyone should think he was doing a Tommy Cooper impression. This, however, only made him look like he was pushing an invisible supermarket trolley. Don't tell him I said so though!

That was the trouble, really. He was far too big to be a successful burglar. He could kick doors in, pull whole window frames out if he wanted, but burglars didn't do that kind of thing. They sort of sneaked around like cats at night and slipped through cracks in windows. So when he had a job to do, he had to bring skinny amateurs in to do the tricky bits. 'If my dad was alive today,' Jimmy moaned, 'he'd turn in his grave!'

He didn't do the burgling at all. He had the know-how alright; a bloody genius when it came to getting into properties. 'That's a Crabbe double-lock, use this,' he'd say, handing you a funny bit of metal. He seemed to have the nerve as well. Either that or he didn't have the sense to be frightened. But I did. That's why I bricked it when he said, 'There's some lead I want – a climbing job, nowt to it – you'll do.' You're probably thinking I should have put my foot down at this point, but the animal eyes fixed me and said, 'Give us an excuse!'

So I found myself that night, freezing in my black polo-neck and balaclava slipping over the railings of a private school. Behind me Jimmy was looking for a gap.

'Wait a minute!' He was hoisting himself awkwardly over a

gate. He poised at the top swaying slightly – with the spikes of the railings threatening to skewer his family jewels – then he leapt and landed heavily on the tarmac playground.

'Bleddy 'ell!' The Pillock had left the sack on the other side. A bloke was walking up the road and I ducked for cover behind a dustbin.

'Pass us that sack, bod!' Jimmy was waving his hand at the man. The man obeyed, and even apologised for not acting promptly enough.

'S'alright,' said the cheeky-daft Jimmy, 'night.'

'What if he calls the coppers? It's too risky now in't it, Jimmy?'

'Nah, he won't . . . not the type. Too bloody helpful by half. He'll goo 'ome thinking how great he is just 'cos he picked the sack up. They're the salt of the earth; my dad reckoned they'd help you to rob their own houses if they could. That is if they ever 'ad owt worth tekkin'.'

I couldn't help suspecting that I was one of these. Why else was I risking life and my neck nicking lead for Jimmy? He'd probably offer a fiver and I'd say, 'Oh no, it's my pleasure,' or summat daft like that. And he'd just slip the fiver in his pocket without a second thought. Of course, what he should have done was force it on me till I accepted it, but Jimmy wasn't brought up like that. If you didn't stick it in your arse pocket straight off, he'd promptly stick it back in his, simple as that.

Anyway, there was still this lead to be got. Jimmy pointed to where the best stuff was. 'It's dead simple. You just roll it up from the bottom: cut it wi' that knife and sling it onto the grass so it don't mek no noise.'

I looked up in the darkness. The roofs of the old school were slippy with recent rain, and a stiff cold wind was ripping the rain clouds up.

'How am I gonna get up there, Jimmy?' I was trembling a bit now.

'Look, don't think about it. You got to get into them valleys where the lead is. Get up the best way you can. If I tell you, you'll only go and get mixed up.'

I started up, found a tree and jumped off that onto a low flat roof. From there, it was easy to get on the slippy slopes of the main roof. Up I went, slowly, slipping back every now and then but moving all the time. Eventually I made the ridge. I felt like Sir Edmund Hilary on the top of Everest. I lit up a fag to celebrate the conquest. 'I did it because it was there, Tensing,' I said to the invisible Sherpa.

'Get a move on you idle get!' Jimmy's voice sailed up to me from below, not a whisper but a full blown yell. Prompted by this, I slithered down the other side of the roof out of sight into the valley made by several melting roofs. The joins were made completely of lead which glowed slightly in the waxing moon. I had conquered Everest and now I had found El Dorado between these mountainous roofs.

Like an old miner from the goldrush days I got the fever. Greedily I hacked at the lead. I was no craftsman; I butchered it unsystematically. It rolled up beautifully and silently. I began to enjoy myself.

'There's gold in the mountains, lead in the valley. . . .' I sang merrily as I worked. Every so often when I got a few rolls together and lobbed them over a wall onto the ground below, they dropped with a pleasant thud. While I was throwing a particularly heavy roll over the edge, I heard Jimmy moaning about something or other; suppose he thought it was too heavy or summat. I worked on regardlessly.

'Come on down . . . Pete . . . come on, that's enough!' The voice was coming from above me. Jimmy had climbed up the roof and was sitting on the ridge waving his arms. He sounded scared; the great Jimmy sounded scared, and there was me, actually enjoying myself! I casually closed the jackknife, I was John Wayne on a commando raid in the heart of Nazi Germany.

'Take it easy, Jim my boy. If a job's worth doing it's worth doin' proper.' On the ridge Jimmy slapped my back and looked at me with what I can only describe as admiration.

'Yer a cool bogger. After what you've just done we should be miles away!'

'What, nicking a bit of lead?'

'No, half killing a copper!' He looked dreamily up at the moon savouring the moment.

'There I was, bagging the lead up and draggin' it out of sight, when up comes a copper. Just there like that, out of the blue, he comes sneaking up. I was in the bushes when I sees him. You was singing and he looked up, like he couldn't believe his eyes. Then I did a daft thing, I bust out laughing. He shone his torch straight at me and I turned to pelt off, but I got tangled up in a bleddy thorn bush: the more I struggled the worse it got. You can imagine how I felt, never been caught in me life and there I wer caught like a bleddy rat in a trap. Anyroad, I hears this thud and turns around as best I could. There he wer laying on the floor with a roll of lead on his back. You was singing away like nowt 'ad 'appened – yer a cool customer!'

I found myself sliding down the roof; suddenly I'd gone all stiff. Jimmy was all for leaving the copper and leggin' it with the lead. In fact that's what he did.

The copper was laying awkwardly on a pile of stones so I carefully moved him and rolled my coat up and put it under his head. His radio crackled and a voice said, 'Thirty-nine. Thirty-nine.' I pressed the little button on the side and told them where he was. Then I cleared off.

The day after, a couple of plain-clothes men came 'round our house. Apparently, my name and address was in the coat I'd put under the copper's head. They tried to get me to tell them who my accomplice was, but I was Jimmy Cagney all day and not a lousy stool-pidgeon, whatever that is. Still, they let me off with a bit of probation, being as it was my first offence.

Jimmy came around the other day as well. He reckons I should set myself up on my own. 'You've got the right temperament,' he said. I think he meant it as well. I didn't do anything to upset his view of me: for one thing it keeps him off my back. But when all said and done, I'm glad I stayed and helped that copper – even if I did get nicked for it – I'm daft like that.

Pete Hannah

■ The human factor ■

Standing here by this machine, hour after hour, all sorts of things come into your head. I'm sure my thoughts spend more time dancing around on the hanger ceiling than they do on the job in hand. That's how human error comes about, what gives them upstairs in that dinky little glass office looking down on us so much trouble. But they can't do anything about that until they design a robot to do what we're doing, which they probably will do one of these days, because if your mind really was on the job in hand you'd drive yourself so mad with boredom you couldn't do the job anyway. So the blokes upstairs just have to accept that, to live with the fact that one in every so many holes plugged in a metal bar's going to be out of synch (roughly the job I've been doing for the past few months), even though it mucks up their columns of figures and spoils their neat little graphs.

You can spot the ones who won't last long straightaway, the ones who can't let their minds drift up to the ceiling while their arms attend to the business in hand. They worry about whether the thing's right or not, instead of getting it out of the way. They've got their sleeves rolled up by ten o'clock, and they're itching all the time, scratching themselves silly. They get angry quickly too, start thumping the machinery when they can't get something straight. It annoys them, and that's it then. Once you let yourself get annoyed, you're letting yourself get involved and that's suicide in this game. How can you get yourself involved in drilling thousands of little holes in pieces of metal eight hours a day? It'd be like doing time and that's exactly how some blokes go through their lives – doing time.

Not me, I just let my thoughts drift up to the ceiling and when I'm down here punching holes in poxy pieces of metal, they're up there pondering the universe as you might say. But mostly it's just the bills or West Ham last Saturday. Sometimes I just look around at the blokes working on the line beside me and think about them.

Take Billy Sullivan, three machines down. We've been neighbours at work and home for over forty years now. (Come to think of it we were in the same class at school as well, desk to desk.) Just to look at him you'd think nothing's happened to him more exciting than the occasional win on the horses. He's got one of those faces you can't call up in your mind when you want to, 'cause there's nothing in his face your memory can get its claws into. It's just another nose, another mouth, another two eyes and ears put near enough each other under a mop of hair to earn the name human. It's the kind of face that makes me suspect that God's a bit like us, up there somewhere punching out people with his mind on something else.

Billy's the kind of bloke things happen to rather than the kind that makes things happen. (Which of the two types lead the most exciting lives is often down to circumstances and pure, blind luck.) 'Cause things have happened to Billy, stone me they have. They just don't seem to register much on his mush.

Take for instance that little matter with Lizzie Kierney. Billy, his face being what it is, wasn't exactly the Don Juan of our area. But he did alright for himself in his quiet, no-fuss way. He hung around, and hung around, and took his chances when they came. One of them was Lizzie Kierney. He saw her, as far as I know, only about three or four times before she was certain and her old dear found out, and her brothers. Bloody hell, Frank, Jack and Steve Kierney – Trouble United. Hard blokes, Jesus, hard as they come, and with as much milk of human kindness as this machine I'm working at. They were Catholics by name: animals by nature. They didn't like their sister being with child out of wedlock.

'Who was it then, Liz?' Frank must've said when he found out, and Lizzie must've answered,

'Can't honestly say, Frank.'

'Can't honestly say. Were you in such a hurry you forgot to ask him his name?'

Funny thing about evil brothers – they expect their sisters to be as pure as the driven snow.

'It's not so much him, Frank,' Lizzie said in that sly way of hers, 'as them.' Well, it turned out that apart from Billy one of the three was a long-distance lorry driver from Glasgow, and the other one was the cook on an Australian freighter, so you don't have be Sherlock Holmes to guess which one of the three they elected to carry the can.

I don't think I even knew at that time that Billy had been seeing Lizzie Kierney. He hadn't talked to me about it, but then he wouldn't. Billy could win the pools and the first you'd know about it would be a postcard from Barbados. (Right enough, if I won the pools that's the first you'd hear of it from me as well.) So first of all, I was a bit displeased by what happened that Sunday afternoon after the boys had tumbled. They never used to drink in the Stag's Head anyway. So that was a bit of a shocker in itself when all three of them waltzed in, Sunday-suit job, and sided up to the bar. But you could've knocked me over with an empty pay-packet (or a full one these days for that matter) when Frank, nestling himself onto a bar stool, suddenly says to the barman,

'And a large scotch for Billy over there.' Billy was every bit as surprised as me by the way he choked on his pint. I wasn't even sure the Kierneys knew who Billy was. Billy smiled a bit in his dozy way as he took the drink.

'What's the occasion, Frank?' I could see he was somewhat nervous by his forced expression. But who wouldn't be with Jack and Steve Kierney casting shadows over each shoulder, and Frank like a crocodile who's just seen his next meal going in for a paddle?

'Wedding,' Steve muttered, swapping shoulders with Jack.

'S'at right?' Billy spluttered. 'One of you lads?' Frank seemed to find that amusing.

'No, no, no, Billy,' he said, his big fat paw slapping the bar-top. He had a hand on him like one of those things they put on the end of a J.C.B.

'Not yet anyway. No, it's Lizzie. The sister.'

'You know Lizzie, Billy, don't you?' Jack said, leaning forward to whisper in Billy's ear.

'I do, yeah. Give her my best wishes.'

'Best wishes. Best wishes,' Frank roared with laughter, pointing at Billy who was trying to look as innocent as possible, sipping his pint. 'He's hilarious. Absolutely hilarious.'

As he said this, he let his hand rest on Billy's shoulder, and then squeezed. I watched it tighten as Billy asked,

'Who's the lucky bloke?'

'You,' Frank said, his face suddenly serious. I thought the hand wasn't going to stop squeezing till the collarbone broke, but it did.

'Welcome to the family,' Steve said.

'Yeah, 'gratulations mate,' Jack added, shaking Billy's limp hand, before it clenched shut and grew white. Then Frank leant over, all pretence of friendliness gone to reveal a face full of grievous bodily harm.

'You should know better than to play around with respectable girls, Billy,' he said, wagging his finger beneath Billy's nose. 'Especially girls from big respectable families.'

I don't know what was going through Billy's brain but he was so rigid he could've taken root. There was a kind of suave arrogance on Frank's face as if he didn't really have to make himself clear to be understood like other people. But there was also a bit of relief in his boat race as well as if somethings had just been settled to the satisfaction of all concerned, even though I could see by Billy's face that it hadn't. Lizzie'd got a husband, the baby a father, and the Kierney's had upheld their status in the community and Frank was happy.

'Now,' he said commandingly, 'after we've finished this you can come back and meet the relations.'

When Billy turned to me he reminded me of what my old man had said about soldiers in the war being shell-shocked. Billy looked as brittle and vulnerable as a chicken bone you could pick up and snap between your thumb and finger. As I said, he was a bit on the dozy side so it'd probably never entered his mind that something like this could happen. When he explained the situation all I could say was,

'Hard luck, mate.' What else could I say? As far as I could see he'd landed himself in it good style. Me and Billy's two of life's small fry. We get pushed this way and that by circumstances beyond our control.

Finally Frank put down his glass – heavily – and put his arm in Billy's as if to accompany him to the door.

'Well, come on, brother-in-law. The future Mrs. Salmon's waiting.'

Well, Billy didn't budge an inch. He didn't. He just stood there with Frank pulling, offering no violence, but firm as a rock. Frank couldn't believe it. He had a gob on him like those people must've had when they saw Jesus turn the water into wine. Billy wasn't pale now, he was flushed with determination. And the stature of him. His backbone was like an upright bar of steel fixed in concrete. Then I saw something about Billy that the Kierneys didn't know him well enough to guess at. He was an obstinate bugger. I remembered the times as kids when someone had picked on Billy and how Billy wouldn't have it, how he'd have taken a certain beating any day than be pushed around. Funny, some people. Anyway, that's more or less what he told Frank when Frank said to him,

'I don't think you understand, Billy boy. You're going to be wed.'

'I'll wed who I want to wed, not who you pick for me.'

I don't think Frank Kierney's ever been talked to like that since his old man died. A funny kind of mad look came over him as he let go of Billy's arm like it was the plague and without a word he marched out of the pub, Bill and Ben the flower-pot men behind him.

'Bloody hell, Billy mate,' I said, 'You've had it now.' Never been much good in a crisis, me.

Next time I saw Billy he was in hospital. Three broken ribs and a face like an Irish spud. He could hardly talk when I got there but he managed to point out the card on the bedside table.

'Get well soon,' it said. 'You'll need all your strength,' signed, 'The Kierneys.'

'I take it you still said no?' I commented. He nodded his head, that was about all he could do.

He was in hospital a month, lucky for him in a manner of speaking, because if he'd have got any better any quicker he'd have been dead – if you see what I mean. You see two things happened in his last weeks in hospital that saved his bacon. Lady Luck smiled on him the way she does sometimes when you're on your last legs. First of all, Lizzie lost the baby falling down the stairs, a sad thing in itself, but it meant that apart from a handful of people nobody knew she was due for one anyway. Then, one thing on another, Frank got done for duffing over the manager of a club downtown and the law came down on him like a ton of bricks and he got three years. While all this was going on, Billy got out of hospital and laid low. After a while he had a sniff outside to see what was happening, but it seemed other things were keeping the brothers occupied.

After a couple of months things had cooled down enough for Billy to get back to normal. Then one day we were in a pub near Waterloo just by chance, a flashier place than we were accustomed to frequent, when who should we bump into but Lizzie Kierney, out with a few of her mates for the night. They were all a bit plastered by the looks of them. I pointed her out to Billy and he looked at her with a kind of interest. I didn't expect him to be bitter, he wasn't that kind of bloke. Then she spotted him and stopped in mid laugh, a glass raised to her lips. She walked towards us through the crowd. Little alarm bells rang in my head ten to the dozen. I gave Billy a tug but he was as stiff as that time in the pub when Frank had tried to pull him.

'Alright, Billy?' she said as she approached, but I didn't have to worry; she wasn't going to stick a glass in his face. She had a sly smile on her, but it was more amused than anything.

'Alright, Lizzie?' Billy replied. 'Sorry about the baby.'

'Oh that's alright,' she said as if she had learnt to live with it. 'I hope it wasn't yours.'

'That doesn't matter.'

'Billy?' she asked, a kind of puzzled look coming on her face.

'Yeah.'

'Why wouldn't you marry me?'

Billy looked at her a minute as if it was something he'd been thinking about himself. He found this much to say about it. He said,

'I didn't like the way your brothers asked me.'

She chewed that one over for a minute as if she didn't quite know how to take it, then said, 'What if I'd have asked you. Would that've made any difference?'

'Might've,' Billy replied cagily.

She seemed to have had enough to mull over for the minute and she went back to her mates. But there was something bugging her and she was soon back again, looking Billy straight in the eye and saying, 'Will you marry me Billy?'

Billy looked at her and replied, 'I don't mind,' and that was how Billy married. Frank Kierney even got a dispensation to get out and attend his sister's wedding. I think he was quite pleased with the bride's choice of partner, the three broken ribs, and accessories conveniently forgotten about.

'Two pints of bitter, barman,' Billy's just shouted across to me 'cause I've got this lever I pull now and again that looks like the pump on a bar. I smile and, what's more fatal, start speeding up with the thought of a pint in my head, as if speeding up can make the time go any quicker. I relax back and Billy catches my eye as if he knows the problem, then he smiles and I smile, and both our thoughts rise up to the ceiling again.

Tom McLennan

Knocking the words into shape

This section consists of ten poems. Each of the poets has wrestled with words, with the power and force and emotional associations of language, to create a poem that expresses an idea within the poetic form they have chosen.

The form of a poem is dictated by the content of the poem, by what the poet is trying to communicate. The shape and sound of a poem – its verse form, its rhythms, its line lengths, its rhyme or non-rhyme – emerge from the content. Thus, a poem such as 'Remember?' which deals with childhood memories, picks up its rhythms and images from the world of childhood, whilst 'For June' which is about a woman reflecting on, and expressing feelings about, her relationship with her mother, has a free vese form, because the poet is exploring less definite ideas, searching for words that will capture her feelings.

Most poems of any worth have to be worked on over a period of time; the poet has to tease out the meaning and the feelings from the words, trying to capture in a phrase, in an image, something true or enlightening. Poetry may depend partly on inspiration, but it relies also on graft and craft. Poems have to be drafted and redrafted and perfected.

The 'imagery' of a poem is very central to its meaning and impact on the reader. Imagery is the collective word for images created by words that appeal to our five senses. The poems 'Child's supper' and 'Job Centre' are especially interesting for the imagery the poets use.

'Kurtin up at Ra Barras', 'The street's gossip' and 'Carnival' create pictures of places and people as does 'Distant sounds', but this poem also tells a dramatic story. Using a public voice, poetry can deal with topical issues directly as in 'Yesterday, today and tomorrow' and 'To you, woman of South Africa'. Indeed, there are few subjects that poetry cannot tackle – the 'magic' consists in ensnaring meaning in a web of language that illuminates experience.

■ Job Centre ■

This is not the Thirties.
The place is bright as lipstick
And well-groomed as the girl
In the swivel chair.
She dizzies round, just for the hell of it,
But, always in control,
Ends firmly facing her typewriter.
Her fingers fit the keys precisely.
A staccato of neat white cards /
Announces what's on offer.
I sidle over, neutrally.
There's nothing there!

Does the Job Library
House fact or fiction?

'Have you registered?'
The question takes me by surprise,
But she is keen to help
So I approach the desk.

She opens a drawer
In the filing-cabinet.
It slides out strong and smoothly.
I half expect to see
A label tied around a cold big toe,
But there are only cards
With names.

Now I'm in there.
At last I have a place.
That's me – a card in a drawer
Marked O to Z.
She shuts it with a satisfying click.

Beth Edge

■ Remember? ■

Remember the days? Now think back hard
To the time when the loo was down the yard,
When you ran a mile to earn a penny
And space invaders? We hadn't any!
The picnics we had with water and butties,
Out in the street for a game of footy –
The bobby would come and chase us away
But still we'd be back the following day.
The walking days, the annual treats
The corner shop where we bought our sweets,
The chewy machine stuck on the wall,
Remember the bobbies? Twelve feet tall!
Remember the houses, all back to back?
Remember the cars, all painted black?
Waiting for tadpoles to turn into frogs,
What were they doing, those two dogs?
Going to school in a gaberdine mac,
Walking it there, running it back,
The dinners were yukky, the milk was free
And all the teachers seemed seventy three.
Wishing your mum would stop making a fuss,
'A penny one please' for a ride on the bus,
Sunday tea when your mum made the cakes –
Remember that bike that had no brakes?
Saturday mornings down at the flicks,
When too many sweets made you feel sick.
Remember shillings and threepenny bits?
Remember the school nurse looking for nits?
Brown football boots, the ball had a lace,
The shorts, that stretched from kneecap to face.
Was all this real or was it a dream?
Were there really trains that ran on steam?
Believe it or not, the answer is yes!
Was it better or worse? It's anyone's guess.

Derek Jones

106

■ For June ■

We were sitting in a cafe
I remember
talking over cigarettes and wine
and suddenly
I saw you as you really are
as you really were
deep through
the woman you show to others
the cocktail smile and quicksilver laugh
of innuendo.

saw you young and girlish
flying eight month's pregnant
cycling through the city's gloom
past the chip shops on the Old Kent Road
the ragtrade sweatshops and newsvendor's stands
with the smell of lemons
on your skin
the flash of Irish blue
in your hair and eyes

saw you warm and milky
holding me in your arms
and laughing
both of us laughing
heads thrown back
to the wind and sun

I took your hand
– or did you take mine?
and it was like a meeting of memories
and of potentials
as though we pushed away
those years of falsity
cut through
the pretence and competition
and I came running in through the backdoor
bursting with stories and poems
came hurtling out of school
clutching paintings and creations
for you
my tender critic
my sharp tongued connoisseur.

Billie Hunter

■ Child's supper ■

A cold mother. A harsh father
The child sits at table
– 'Tell your father I've had enough' –
– 'Tell your mum, she'd better shut up' –
The child slides under the table
    This is the way the world goes round
    Under the table, you can't hear a sound

A cold mother. A harsh father
Their legs are under the table
The lino is pretty with roses bright red
But you can't pick them. The flowers are dead
    Under the table, there isn't a sound
    And nothing, nothing at all goes round

A cold mother. A harsh father
If only the table had a hole
One could crawl through it like a mole
'I'm blind, I'm dumb
Please give me a crumb!'
    But under the table, there's no air and no sound
    And suddenly everything goes round
    The child is sick under the table

Then there is rushing
And flushing
And holding
And scolding
And slamming of doors
And scrubbing of floors
And where the roses been before
The lino is ripped clean off the floor
And: 'Tell your mum she's done that well' –
And: 'Tell your father to go to hell' –
And, at last, disgraced, unfed,
Hungry to bed
    But father and mother have made it up
    Go to the pub.

Lotte Moos

■ Kurtin up at Ra Barras ■

Kimeer, haw bit kimeer,
An' see this ah've goat here.
It's really gorgeous curtain stuff,
Youse niver seen afore.
Liz Taylor's goat it in 'er lounge
(Tell that tae hurr next door).

Kimeer! Kimeer!
Don't go away, kimeer.
Anither bit, the very same!
An' since ah know yurr thrifty
Though ah could get a coupla quid,
Tae you, it's jist WAN FIFTY!

Whit's up wi yiz?
Who-r izzit toarn?
Och, naebuddy'll see.
Jist pleat it so's it wullny show.
Who'll gimme FIFTY P.?

Speak up a wee bit louder, Hen.
The pattern's aw squinty?
That's jist the wey ah'm haudin' it up,
For you . . . ah'll make it TWINTY.

Nae use? Aw well, forget it –
Since it needs a bitta stitchin'
Jist gie it tae that wee auld wife.
(It'll dae furr hurr wee kitchen.)

Ten yards o' screenin' – SIXTY P.
Noo that's a bargain, 'int it?
Ye get the "durty' bits furr free.
Well, you could always tint it.

Here's a wee bit wi' a frilly edge,
It's aw ah've left o' this.
Ye hivny oany money, Maw?
Awright then, geez a kiss.

That's the lot! Noo ah'm gon hame,
Ah'm fairly oot o' puff, an'
Ah've only goat some oad bits left.
Here, catch them! THURR FURR NUTHIN!

Isabelle Gorra

■ The street's gossip ■

Hello there love, it's only me,
Ada, from across the way.
I thought I'd come and help you
Pass the time of day.

Young John Brown is back 'inside'
And Doreen's done a bunk.
She's left her kids with her mother,
The bloke she's run off with's a punk.

Old Fred Smith's won some brass
His horses won, let's see,
They were Blacky, Jepson and Winsome Lass
Ten-to-one all three.

Hey, t'milkman's gone in that house,
He's after that young lass June –
He'd better get his skates on
'Cause her hubby will be home soon.

Well, I'd best get going now, love,
I've got to make Alf's tea,
You'll natter on till day ends,
Ya should be quiet, love, like me.

Mary Whittaker

■ Carnival ■

In this window
Set high
In a wall
We sit and watch
The carnival
Passing us by
On the street below.
Then (strangely dreamlike)
You rise from your chair
(Letting fall my hand)
And descend to the door
Which leads on to the street
Where all of the other dancers
(In their faded costumes)
Have also come to stand
And beckon me down.

Kevin Otoo

■ Distant sounds ■

Old McGroder moved out of the maw of the night
Riding shotgun on a rick of hay.
He urged the ailing beast homeward
With talk and the butt of a pitchfork.
'The last of the horsemen,' my father'd said.

But in my dreams he rode instead
Bent on pillage to the nearby parish
Of Magheracloone.

I heard him grunt, and his old adversary
'The Tare McMahon' launched a wad
Of well-chewed tobacco against a wall.

A skein of geese broke and scudded
Along the ridge of Gartlans bog.

The moon emerged and cut a swathe
Of alabaster light down our street,
As I heard for the first time
Those sounds of discord
Sounds of hate
Waft south across the lake,
Like the muffled dip of a poacher's oar
Or furniture tossed about a distant room.

Headlined in the next day's paper:
'R. U. C. BARRACKS LAID WASTE'.

Peter Woods

■ Yesterday, today, tomorrow ■

Yesterday I was younger,
Yesterday I believed
That God watched over the world at large,
That real dairy butter was better than marg,
That the good guys were good and the bad guys were bad,
That no-one in power could really be mad,
That a friend in need was a friend indeed,
That only women bleed.

But today I've seen it all, and now I know better.

Today I am
anti-rich and anti-poor,
anti-you lot having more,
anti-pigeons, anti-cars,
anti-shuttle-trips to Mars,
anti-nuclear power,
anti-news on the hour,
anti-Thatcher, anti-Reagan,
anti-Hitler, anti-Begin,
anti-'O' levels and CSEs,
anti-intellectuals with Economy degrees,,
anti-yellow phoneboxes, and red ones, too,
anti-paying in public loos,
anti-drink and anti-drugs,
anti-Charles and Diana mugs,
But tomorrow . . .

Tomorrow I'll give up,
I won't try to change the world,
I will realise, acknowledge and accept.
I won't show surprise when the leader I'm following lies
And I won't know how to reject.
Tomorrow I'll watch telly while I'm eating my lunch,
And if they show a little violence – who cares?
I'll be a Conservative but think I'm a radical,
I'll sit back and enjoy the decline,
I'll shop at Safeway's or Tesco's or Spar,
Rip up yours to make mine.
Tomorrow the apathy sets in,
And I'll welcome it, sit back and grin,
I'll paint my toenails with Mary Quant,
I'll do whatever they think I want.

Maureen Miles

■ For you, woman of South Africa ■

You live under the wide horizon of Africa
Under her wildness of deserts and mountains
And in the night you hear the roll of the ocean

You live under a killing sun
In a shantytown called Crossroads
And you are waiting for a home
    Day after day
        year
           after
              year

Woman of South Africa
You want to live
On your land, in your city, in your street and your home
But THEY want to crush you and doom you
And you are sweeping the sand in the desert
    Day after day
        year
           after
              year

They took away your husband
To use his strength for their wealth
They took you away from your children from
    Dawn
        to
        dusk
Woman of South Africa
One morning, you woke up in anger and pain
And you shouted at the killing sun
And your friends and sisters woke up with you
Together you uttered the deep cry of South Africa

And together you clenched your fist
Together you started to fight
When they put you into prison
Despite despair, despite hunger
Despite your children dying
You only grew stronger

What strength lies in your heart!
What hope lies in your eyes!
Still sweeping the sand in the desert
You live from day to day
    from hour to hour
    from minute to minute

For the struggle of your people
    a struggle for justice
    a struggle for liberty
    a struggle for victory
Until the day you will be free and you will rise
Embracing the whole wide horizon of South Africa

Anneliese Klock

Follow on

■ Writers' workshops

All the pieces in this anthology were first published by community publishers based in many parts of Britain. Community publishers usually publish writing by non-professional writers in local areas. These local writers do their writing as members of local community writing workshops or projects. These workshops depend on local people coming together because of their common interest in writing and the collaborative spirit that is always a feature of this kind of activity. Collaboration among the writers involves sharing of ideas, mutual encouragement and interest in one another's creative output.

For discussion:

Here are some relevant quotes from the introductions to some of the publications which are represented in this book:

'I started writing when I was seven, complicated fantasies and adventure stories. My eccentric nicotine-stained and wonderful English teacher scrawled over one composition, "Write about what you know. Why do you have to turn everything into a fantasy?" At 18 I left school and trained to become a nurse and midwife. I left fantasy life behind, and for ten years worked in the realms of nitty-gritty reality. My writing was buried. At 29 things began to change fast. My shell of defences was blown apart and I began to write again. This time the words were different. I wanted to write about the real world, about ordinary women's experiences.'
   Billie Hunter, author of 'For June'.

'To get the discussion and writing going we made a collection of photos and articles from newspapers, magazines and books, local statistics on births and hospital facilities, poems and songs on child-birth, old sayings and customs. This we made into a wall display. We arranged for two midwives to come and talk about their work and exchange ideas. We talked about many different aspects of childbirth. We learned about customs in other countries and about hospital practices.'
   Introduction to *Every Birth is Different*, a collection of writing about the experience of childbirth from which 'It was really great when Jaye was born' was taken.

'If I didn't live in Hackney but on a lonely moor, I might have concentrated on moorhens. But . . . from behind the walls came voices asking the writer to bear witness.'
   Lotte Moos, author of 'Child's supper'.

'In a short time, we were able to build up a feeling of trust and support for each other, so much so that individual fears and inhibitions subsided, our confidence grew and we were able to develop and experiment with different aspects of writing.'

Anne Gebbett, author of 'A change of heart'.

'Publication begins when two or three gather together to get a message across, and in practice it is more exciting to hear new words from a person you thought you knew than to read a page of an author who exists only by name. The text is transformed by a live presence – by accent, image and proximity. Feelings can be registered face to face; we can extrapolate where writing falls short, and answer back.'

Introduction to *Sheets in the Wind*, the collection from which 'Victorian piece' was chosen.

'Women have been writing about their lives and experiences as far back as writing began, but without female critics or publishers, most of their works were doomed to obscurity. Our efforts, written and published by women, will help break through the silence surrounding us and will encourage other women to try something similar. After all, if you can talk, you can write.'

Introduction to *If you can talk, you can write* the collection from which 'The confirmation class' was taken.

Do-it-yourself publishing

Within your own class
Aim to produce class anthologies of writing from time to time, perhaps once a term; everybody in the group should be represented in the anthology by at least one piece.

Methods of production
The simplest method is by writing your pieces on carbon, then running off copies on a duplicating machine. Staple them together. If a roneo machine or even an off-set litho is available, the production of short booklets should not be complicated. Using a photocopier to produce copies of each piece is more expensive but very easy. This method is most suitable if you are aiming at a limited print run.

Illustrations
Negotiate with Art teachers for time within art lessons to provide illustrations for your writing and/or anthologies.

Writers' Club
Start a writers' club for your year or the whole school. Advertise it round the school and do not be discouraged if only a few turn up to begin with. Once established, it will become part of school life.

Visiting authors

Invite favourite authors to visit your school. If there is a school bookshop, organise discussions of favourite books and authors, and run practical writing workshops. Aim to produce booklets of writing produced from these sessions.

Talking and writing

If you can talk, you can write is the title of one community writing anthology. Talking is an important preparation for writing. It is useful for:

- exchanging initial ideas;
- sharing common experiences;
- collaborating in writing;
- acting as helpful critics of each other's writing;

Brainstorms

Class brainstorms are a useful means of pooling ideas for writing. When topics for writing are being decided, have a session of 'brainstorming' and list ideas on the blackboard. Sometimes sharing ideas in small groups or one-to-one co-operation is preferable to class brainstorms.

Using tape

Some of you may like to make a tape recording of what you are going to write about as a first step before you put pen to paper; from the tape you can write an edited transcript. This means:
1. listen to the tape and decide what you want to use;
2. edit the words, cutting out things you have said clumsily or repetitively;
3. write a first draft;
4. discuss this draft with classmates and/or a teacher;
5. do a second draft.

Sharing

The idea of sharing is central to community writing. As often as possible, pool and share your ideas with friends. Read over each other's work; act as the audience or readership.

Make helpful suggestions to improve each other's writing:
Is the opening to that story interesting enough?
Is there a clear narrative line?
Is the pace of the writing just right?
Are the arguments of the piece clear to the reader?
Does the piece have an effective ending?
How realistic and effective is the direct speech?
Can the accuracy (spelling, sentence construction, punctuation, grammar) be improved?

Some writing games

Making lists

Share your ideas for these simple, light-hearted writing tasks.
Sometimes making lists can help you with ideas for pieces of
continuous writing. Here are some lists you can make:
   The Top Ten jobs you would most like/hate to do;
   Your Top Ten all-time favourite words;
   Your Top Ten ways of passing time;
   Your all-time Top Ten records;
   Your all-time Top Ten favourite TV programmes;
   Your Top Ten places/foods/drinks

Send-ups

Writing parodies, spoofs or send-ups can be fun. Here are some
suggestions:
   send-up soap operas, sports commentaries, agony aunt problem
   pages, politicians' speeches, radio or TV interviews with guest
   celebrities, news bulletins, disc jockey programmes and weather
   forecasts;
   make up mock crosswords or quizzes, crazy inventions;
   parody school reports and school notices.

Writing stories together

As a group of three or four, decide on a topic for a story. Each of
you take it in turns to contribute a sentence to the narrative. When
it is your turn, you have to continue from the point in the narrative
where the previous person has left you.

Everyday sayings

Make a list of everyday sayings you have heard people say. Then
consider which would make a suitable starting-point for a narrative.

Drama improvisation

Very often acting out a play or scene in small groups will stimulate
your imagination and show you how to approach a particular theme
in writing.

Working towards a final version

Very few pieces of writing come out just right in the first draft. Most
writers – community writers and professional writers, such as
journalists and novelists – always write a first draft, then edit and
correct this draft before submitting it for publication. In your own writing,
try to get into the habit of working your way through these stages:
   1. generate ideas through talking/sharing/brainstorms;
   2. sort ideas out into skeleton or outline form;
   3. write a first draft;
   4. discuss this draft with your friends/teacher;

5. edit the first draft. Look for ways of cutting out irrelevant sections, add things you have omitted, improving the expression and the accuracy of your writing, reshaping the structure of the piece.
6. write a second draft;
7. 'proof-read': professional writers receive page proofs from publishers before the piece is sent off to be printed; you should read the 'proofs' of your writing before finally submitting it for assessment.

■ Keeping a personal record

This section may have started you thinking about your own life. Here are some ways of helping you to jog your memory.

Family albums
1. Bring in to school some family photographs, including some of yourself at various ages: as a baby, at the time you started primary school etc. In small groups exchange these photos.
2. Construct a family tree based on your own family:

Frank Jones = Emma Smith

Margaret   Joseph   George = Violet Brown

3. Make an album of family photographs and under each photo write a brief sketch in words of each of the relatives in the picture.

Diaries
Keep a diary or journal to express your feelings, to record daily events and to note down thoughts or observations as they come to you. Take time in English lessons to write in your journal from time to time. Make it clear to others and to your teacher, whether or not you want this journal to be private or not.

Working in pairs
1. Use a cassette recorder for oral activities in pairs. With a friend recall memories of childhood: interesting anecdotes about people, places, unusual incidents, surprises, frights, triumphs, disasters, happy days, sad days, holidays and primary school experiences.
2. Co-operate in writing a film script about each other's life. Remember film is mainly a visual medium so you must write down what you want the camera to show:
    Scene 5 Outside Primary School gates.

Me arriving with Mum on my first day at primary school.
Camera close-up of my anxious face looking around to see
if I can see any of my friends.
I see a friend and rush up to her/him.
3. Create a life chart for each other in which you plot the most
important events of your lives:

17th August 19—:   Born at Forester Hospital at 9.20 a.m.;
weighed 7lbs 6oz.

19—:   First memory: looking through the bars
of my cot.

16th September 19—:   Started Eaglesfield Primary School.

Leave space to add drawings and photographs that illustrate
important events in your life chart.

Class brainstorms

As a class, share experiences from the past that could be used as
material for writing. Here are some suggestions to prompt your
memories:

nursery school;
childhood illnesses;
first day at junior school;
special events e.g. birthdays,
celebrations, family
occasions;
holidays;
making friends;
quarrels;
getting into trouble;
fairs and markets;
going to the pictures;
favourite telly programmes from
the past;
books read over and over again;
comics and magazines;
fears and panics;
changing schools;
moving house;
losing friends/making new
friends;
fights;
falling out with parents;
gangs/rivalries/bullying;
youth organisations (e.g.
brownies, guides, cubs,
scouts);
street games/chants/songs;
collecting things;

strange characters you
remember;
hideaways/secret places;
pets;
summer evenings;
storms/snow;
camps/outdoor pursuits;
sporting triumphs/ disasters;
being a fan (of a band/team);
part-time jobs (e.g. paper round);
clothes;
records;
favourite toys;
adventures and scrapes;
accidents;
embarrassing experiences;
tests/examinations;
in disgrace;
famous events you remember;
times you got lost;
journeys/big cities;
chores you hated/liked doing;
things you made/couldn't make;
misunderstandings (e.g. of
words, of adult behaviour);
childhood hobbies/ pastimes;
leaving primary school;
family cars/bikes you owned;

Suggestions for written work

1. Interview a relative or someone else you know who has recently given birth. Do a recording of the interview and then use that as the starting-point for a 'human interest' article that you have been asked to write for a young people's magazine.
2. 'Happy days, sad days'. Write an account of some vivid days from your childhood, some of which hold happy memories and others rather sad ones.
3. We can all remember particular times in our younger days when we experienced disappointment in some way, e.g. the time when we finally realised the truth about Santa Claus or when we failed a test of some kind. Write about some of those times.
4. 'Letting people down'. All of us have felt guilty at times because we think we have let someone down in some way. Write about times when you felt like that.
5. 'He/she was an odd individual'. Write a story about a young person who is unusual in some way, but to whom you, as the author, feel some sympathy.
6. 'Coming to England'.
7. 'The fair'. Write a descriptive piece about a fair that came to your area.
8. 'Don't stop the Carnival'. Write a story or poem with this title.
9. 'Holidays I remember'.
10. 'Primary School memories'.
11. Write an account of childhood illnesses you endured, describing how you felt at the time and how they appear from the vantage point of the present.
12. 'Fears I have grown out of.'
13. 'Leaving it all behind'. Write about a time when you moved house, changed school or went through some other similar change in your life.
14. 'Bullying'. Write an account of any bullying you have encountered and express your opinions about the best way to deal with this problem.
15. 'Secrets'. Write a piece about secrets that you used to share as a child with a few friends but kept from other people. e.g. a secret code or language.
16. 'Childhood games'. Write an account of the street games you used to play as a child, including any rhymes, chants or songs associated with them.
17. 'I was a fan of . . .'. Write a piece about yourself as a fan when you were much younger.
18. 'Embarrassing experiences'. Write about embarrassing experiences you had when you were a child, that still make you blush to this very day!

19. 'Success and failure'. Write about one occasion when you were successful in achieving something you were aiming for and one occasion when you failed to achieve some goal you had set for yourself.
20. 'I got lost!'
21. Write about some of your favourite toys you remember from childhood.
22. 'Teachers'. Write about some of the teachers you remember who taught you before secondary school.
23. 'The new pupil'. Write about a time when you started a new school. How did you feel?
24. 'I remember that day when . . .' Recall what you were doing on the day when some famous event took place, e.g. some special event in your area or a national occasion of some kind.
25. 'Summing it up'. Write a piece that sums up your life so far, expressing your feelings about the past and about the future as well.

Further reading

Chunia Achebe   *Things Fall Apart* (Heinemann Educational)
Stan Barstow   *Joby* (Heinemann Educational)
Simone de Beauvoir   *Memories of a Dutiful Daughter* (Penguin)
Anita Desai   *The Village by the Sea* (Puffin)
Buchu Emecheta   *Second Class Citizen* (Fontana)
Ann Frank   *The Diary of Ann Frank* (Pan)
Maxim Gorki   *My Childhood* (Penguin)
Laurie Lee   *Cider with Rosie* (Penguin); *As I walked out one midsummer morning* (Penguin)
Shiva Naipaul   *Beyond the Dragon's Mouth* (Sphere)
V S Naipaul   *Miguel Street* (Heinemann Educational)
Rukshana Smith   *Sumitra's Story* (MacMillan)
Mildred Taylor   *Roll of Thunder, hear my cry* (Gollancz)
Alice Walker   *The Color Purple* (Women's Press)
Richard Wright   *Black Boy* (Penguin)

■ Capturing the moment

If you have taken up the suggestion made on page 00 about keeping a journal or diary, you may be able to use some of the incidents you note in your journal as the starting points for pieces of expressive writing. The five pieces in this section of the anthology all try to capture moments in the writers' lives that were particularly important to them:

In 'Moment', the author writes of a tremendous feeling of satisfaction with his work as a bricklayer.

In 'Cruelty on a summer's day', the writer expresses a feeling of sadness at man's cruelty; this emotion arises from one particular incident.

In 'The rest is history', the writer makes the contrast between the creative act of baking and the news bulletin full of potential mass destruction.

In 'Helen', the subject is a brief encounter with a lonely and outcast individual.

In 'Jack at the Palace', the writer describes the failure of a performer in attempting to win over a hostile audience.

Keeping a log

As an alternative to keeping a diary or journal, write a log of interesting things or incidents that you see around you. Do not keep this on a daily or regular basis: record only events that strike you as interesting or odd. Professional writers often do this: jotting down notes of little incidents they observe which they think they might use later in their writing. The incidents do not need to be very dramatic; for example, they could be like these:

an unexpected act of kindness or cruelty you observe;

a chance encounter with a stranger (e.g. a down-and-out, a lonely, old person);

a feeling of satisfaction you get from doing something really well;

something you listen to on the radio or see on television that sets off a train of thought or triggers memories;

an incident in the street (e.g. a quarrel, people meeting each other, friends chatting);

a dramatic incident (an accident, a fight, police cars with sirens blaring);

peaks of happiness (e.g. at a disco, a party or on a sporting occasion);

depths of despair (sudden disappointments, the blues);

moments of loneliness;

the impact of your surroundings on your moods;

the changes in the weather and its effect on your mood;

missing someone close to you;

moments of irritation;

feelings of frustration;

times when you feel anything is possible;

times when you feel trapped;

time passing slowly.

Record these types of incidents and feelings in a log. Then, if you wish to, choose some of them as topics for pieces of continuous writing. Try to capture the moment in your writing.

Biography

In the section 'Keeping a personal record' we were discussing autobiographical writing, i.e. you writing about your own life and experience. Biographical writing is writing about someone else's life and experiences. In small groups or in pairs, make a list of people you know, who might make interesting subjects for biographical writing, e.g. relatives, neighbours, old people.

Conducting an interview

From the list you make, narrow your choice down and make arrangements to interview the person or persons you have chosen. Make a definite appointment with the people concerned; don't just turn up and hope they will be able to give you their time. Prepare some questions and background notes about the topics you are going to discuss. Here are some possible areas of interest:

changes in the local area from when they were young;
vanishing local landmarks e.g. cinemas, theatres, street markets;
their past working lives;
redevelopment of the area: what do they think of it?
community spirit and sense of belonging;
how they spent their leisure time when they were teenagers;
wartime memories;
memories of hard times;
children's games they used to play;
the comparison of young people's freedom nowadays with 'their day';
crime in the area: has it become worse?;
old customs and traditions of the area;
changes in the local transport system;
supporting the local football team in the old days;
special celebrations in the area e.g. VE Day, the Coronation, the year they won the cup;
going to the pictures in years gone by;
holidays: what kind? where? day trips?
schools and schooldays: how have they changed?
getting into trouble in their youth;
housing conditions in the old days;
special treats;
Christmas/religious festivals;
street games/children's chants from the past;
old photographs of the area;
fashions in their day;
who were their idols?

129

Starting to write

Once you have recorded your interview(s) or made notes of the interview(s), select what you think is most relevant and interesting, i.e. edit the interviews and write your biographical pieces with an introduction and perhaps comment/reflections from you, the biographer. Add photographs where possible.

Looking elsewhere

To help you with your biographical writing, you could consult any of the following in your local area:

    your local library, especially the local history section;
    local museums;
    community publishing projects;
    charity organisations, such as Age Concern;
    the archives of the local newspaper.

Further reading

Maya Angelou	*I know why the caged bird sings* (Virago)
Alan Ayckbourn	*Ernie's Incredible Illucinations* (play) (French)
Alan Bleasdale	*The Boys from the Blackstuff* (Hutchinson)
Bill Forsythe	*Gregory's Girl* (play) (CUP)
Harper Lee	*To Kill a Mocking Bird* (Penguin)
David Leland	*Flying into the Wind, Tales out of School* (CUP)
Bernard MacLaverty	*Secrets and other Stories* (Allison and Busby)
Stephen Poliakoff	*City Sugar* (play) (French)

■ Telling a story

Here and now

' "For those in peril" ' and 'The confirmation class' are both examples of narrative fiction based on the experience and observation of the authors. How 'true' the story is, is not relevant; it does not matter whether the incidents described happened or not. What matters is how authentic the story seems to the reader.

' "For those in peril" ' and 'The confirmation class' are almost certainly based on the authors' own experience or memories of incidents during their schooldays. The approach is 'realistic', i.e. the school setting of the stories is realistically described: the assembly, the classroom scenes, the pupils' reactions to the inspection, the punishment, the way the teachers are described.

■ Writers' workshop 1 ■
Finding a 'peg' for your stories

Most successful short stories take as their starting-point one
incident or theme:
in ' "For Those in Peril" ' it is the school inspection of hands;
in 'The confirmation class' it is the importance of the
confirmation dress in the girl's life.
—These are the 'pegs' on which the stories hang. Very often
it is useful to find a 'peg', an idea, incident or short theme
on which to hang your narrative. Remember these guidelines
for your short-story writing:
   1. Do not try to pack your short stories with too much plot
       or too many incidents.
   2. Build your story round a plot or incident that can be
       handled adequately within the length of a short story.

There is more to the stories than just 'plot', however. The
pegs on which each of the stories hang allow the authors
the opportunity to express something about school life say,
or authority and injustice. The authors use their plots to
express something more general about life and human
behaviour.

Suggestions for written work
Choose any of the suggestions below as pegs for stories with a
school setting. In telling your story try to express something you feel
is important about the experience of school.

1. A young person is involved in an incident at school which leaves
    him or her with a strong sense of injustice. Write a story
    describing the incident and its aftermath: the feelings of the young
    person, what this person does about the injustice and whether
    or not the situation is resolved.
2. 'The Punishment'.
3. 'I suddenly realised that there was a human being behind the front
    this teacher wore.' Write a story with this sentence as its ending.
4. Write a story, based on actual experience but fictionalised, about
    a humorous incident at school.
5. 'They called me a goody-good!' Write a story about a pupil whose
    friends turn against her/him because they suspect her/him of
    being a 'goody-good'.
6. 'The Model Pupil'.

131

The family

Both ' "D for Dad" ' and 'Letting go' are about family life and the relationships within families. In both pieces, the authors explore the feelings of their characters; the real theme of ' "D for Dad" ' is the feelings the child has about her absent father and about her sister and mother.

■ Writers' workshop 2 ■
Viewpoint

' "D for Dad" ' is seen largely from the viewpoint of a young child. 'Letting go' is seen from the viewpoint of an anxious mother. In story-telling you have to decide from whose viewpoint the story is being told. It may be that of:
   a first person narrator, who may or may not be the same character as the author;
   a third person narrator who remains outside the story (i.e. a person who is not directly involved in the action him/ herself but represents the author's voice or presence;
   mainly the viewpoint of one character in the story;
   the viewpoint of two or more characters in the story.

You, the writer, choose the viewpoint of the story and you should have a clear idea from whose standpoint you are telling a story before you start writing it.

■ Writers' workshop 3 ■
Creating a storyline

Most authors create an outline of their stories before they start. They try to avoid unnecessary preambles or irrelevant sections. You can call these outlines 'skeleton plots' or storylines. The storyline for ' "D for Dad" ' might have looked like this:
   1. establish war-time background and Ellen's feelings about her Dad;
   2. the new baby and Ellen's mother;
   3. incident of hiding from her mother;
   4. tea: Bernie and her mother complain about her;

5. in her room: fantasies about treasure;
6. the air-raid warden and her mother's anger;
7. her decision to run away;
8. the planes overhead: D-Day and 'D for Dad';
9. the family united again

This storyline is sufficient to provide a clear narrative thread. In the writing of the story, the writer has 'fleshed it out' with description, by entering into her character's thoughts and by using direct speech.

Suggestions for written work

Create storylines or skeleton plots for as many of the writing suggestions below as you like. The ideas revolve round families or family life. Once you have created your storylines, choose those you think have most potential for successful story writing and write the complete versions.

1. Write a story about a family with an 'absent' parent. In your story try to explore the emotional effect of this absence on the members of the family.
2. 'The Return'. Use this title for a story about family life.
3. 'A Family Occasion'. Write a story based on the idea of an important family occasion of some kind.
4. 'My parents just don't understand me, that's all there is to it!' Write a story with this as its opening.
5. Write a story about the tensions caused between a young person and his/her parent or parents about how much freedom he/she should be allowed.

The community

The next four stories reach out beyond the family circle to the community or the community, represented by certain figures of authority, enters the life of the family.

In 'The Visitor' the unexpected visitor is a Catholic priest.

In 'Death came to dinner', authority is represented by two police officers.

'Thank Gawd for the National Health' looks at an individual's encounter with the Welfare State.

'First steps to the last' records the impact of the depression of the 30s on one family.

Dialogue

Each of the four stories uses direct speech: the actual words characters say. Direct speech is one option open to you as story-teller; putting down the actual words that characters say helps to dramatise events in stories.

■ Writers' workshops 5 ■
Dialect

Each of the four stories has local dialect words in the direct speech. The authors aim to reproduce the colloquial, everyday speech of people living in the local area.

In your own story-telling you could aim to use local dialect in the direct speech. This may well help the realism of your stories and help establish the local setting.

Suggestions for written work
a. Recording dialect

Perhaps you may not be very familiar with the way dialect words you know and use look when written down. As an exercise, improvise in pairs short scenes based on any of the situations listed below. Record the dialogue, which should partly be in your local dialect, and then play it back, listening carefully to the way the dialect words sound. Then transcribe at least part of the dialogue, listening carefully to the sound of the dialect words and spelling them as they sound.

Here are some suggestions for improvisation:

two local farmers meet in a cattle market and pass the time of day;

two supporters of the local football team discuss their team's prospects in an important game;

two neighbours chat across the garden fence about local events;

two people waiting a long time for a bus discuss local services;

two young people chat about how to spend their Saturday night;

a parent tells off her/his teenage daughter/son about the state of her/his room.

Writing a story

1. 'When I opened the door and saw who it was, I froze on the spot.' Use this sentence as the opening for a story.
2. 'The Protest Meeting'. Write a story about a public meeting held in your local area to protest about a local issue.
3. 'Thank goodness for the . . .'. Add the final words of the title yourself and write a story based on the completed title.
4. Write a story based on the idea of a young person coming into contact with some figure of authority in your local area. The contact can hostile or friendly, helpful or unhelpful; as the author you can decide!
5. 'The Depression'. Write a story set in your local area in which your characters suffer from the results of hard times/economic depression.
6. 'Helping one another out'. Write a story, again set in your local area, in which people help one another in some way when problems arise.

The workplace

Four of the stories in this section: 'A man like Mulloy', 'A change of heart, 'Nothing surprised me at Grumpton's' and 'The water rats' are set against a background of the workplace: a building site, a newspaper office, a factory and a coal mine. All four authors had direct, first-hand experience of working in these various workplaces before they came to write their stories. In your own writing try to use your own experience, the backgrounds and settings you know well, e.g.

   school/college   part-time employment   your local area

You can also draw upon what you have learnt from past experiences, the experience of friends and relatives, and your understanding or experience gained from reading fiction, which uses workplaces as settings, and films about work.

Suggestions for written work

1. 'My first day at the new job'. Write a story with this title or an account based on personal experience.
2. 'He/she had it in for me from the moment I started work there.' Use this sentence as the opening to a story about work.
3. 'The Competitors'. Write a story with this title, based on the idea of two people who become very competitive with one another at work.
4. 'The Boss'.
5. 'I had never thought much about trade unions until that day.' Write a story with this conclusion.
6. Write a story about a young person who starts a new job and gradually changes his/her attitude to it, e.g. from liking it to hating it, or *vice versa*.

135

Other times, other places

'Victorian piece' is set in the middle of the 19th century. The author has not written a story based on his own experience or any living person's experience. The story, characters and setting have had to be wholly imagined and recreated. However, the author reveals in the story that he knew something about the period in which the story is set:

army recruiting methods of the time ('taking the shilling');
social conditions (poverty, large families, very cramped living conditions;)
the historical background (the Crimean War).

Sometimes when a writer invents a story it is difficult to be certain whether the events really happened or not. 'Jimmy takes the lead' and 'The human factor' are stories like these. They could be accurately described as 'slices of life'. The stories are set against a realistic background – community life, the workplace – and they are told in a racy colloquial, almost light-hearted style.

■ Writers' workshop 6 ■
Narrative style

Both stories use a colloquial narrative style. The first person narrators tell their stories 'in character', i.e. something of their personalities comes over in the way they tell their stories. The tone is chatty, confidential and colloquial. We learn a lot about the narrators' attitudes to work, to authority, and to the characters in their stories. The first person narrators in these stories are not neutral observers; they take sides and they have a definite presence in the stories.

Suggestions for written work
a. Recreating the past

In pairs make a list of past times that are of particular interest to you. From your knowledge of, or research about, one of these periods, make a short list of characteristic features of the time that might act as starting-points for a story.

The period you can choose to set your story in need not be in the distant past. It could be in the 1960s or 1970s, for example, but in your story try to communicate something about the time to your readers.

Here are some ideas:
some famous local event (e.g. a battle, a disaster);
a period of great hardship (e.g. a time of famine or mass
unemployment);
a famous local historical figure;
the time of a great local triumph.

b. Writing a first person narrative

Choose any of the following topics to write about, using first person
narrative to write your stories. The narrator's personality should
come over in the narrative style you choose to use.
1. 'I was caught fair and square. I couldn't talk my way out of it.'
   Write a story with this opening.
2. Write a story about a young person who is persuaded to do
   something illegal by another young person with a very persuasive
   personality.
3. 'I take orders from nobody!' Write a story with this title.
4. 'Getting out of a fix!'
5. 'He/she was trouble with a capital T'. Write a story with this
   opening sentence.

Further reading

Ranjana Ash	Short Stories from Pakistan, India and Bangladesh (Nelson)
Stan Barstow	The Desperadoes and other Stories (Corgi)
Marjorie Darke	A Long Way to Go (Puffin)
Lewis Grassic Gibbon	A Scots Quair (Pan)
Graham Greene	Brighton Rock (Penguin)
Susan Hill	Strange Meeting (Longman); A little bit of Singing and Dancing (Penguin)
Minfong Ho	Rice without Rain (Deutsch)
George Lamming	The Emigrants (Allison and Busby)
Doris Lessing	This was the Old Chief's Country (Collected African stories Volume 1); The Habit of Loving (Panther and Triad/Grafton Books)
Earl Lovelace	The Dragon can't dance (Longman)
ed. Marland	Caribbean Stories (Heinemann)
Carson McCullers	The Heart of a Lonely Hunter (Penguin)
Ngugi	The River Between (Heinemann)
Edna O'Brien	The Girl with Green eyes (Penguin); The Love Object and other stories (Penguin)
Robert O'Brien	Z for Zachariah (Heinemann)
J D Salinger	The Catcher in the Rye (Penguin)
Samuel Selvon	The Lonely Londoners
Alan Sillitoe	Saturday Night and Sunday Morning
Ngugi Wa Thiong'a	Petals of Blood

■ Knocking the words into shape

The writing of poetry requires craft *and* graft. You do need inspiration as well: something must set you off wanting to write a poem, *but* creating the poem, knocking the words into shape, means you will have to draft and redraft and draft again before you are satisfied with it. Very few poems come out just as you want them at first.

Sometimes it is best to leave a draft of a poem you have written and come back to it a day or so later. In writing poetry you are trying to express something – feelings, an experience, an idea – in a web of language. You have to wrestle with the sounds and meanings of words to get it just as you want it.

Poetry and personal experience

A lot of people use poetry as a way of writing about experiences in their lives that have been important to them either because they were particularly intense or because they were very private or both. In 'Remember?' and 'For June', the poet evokes childhood memories with affection. With 'Child's supper', the mood changes.

■ Writer's workshop 1 ■
Rhyme

You may want to use rhyme in your poems to emphasise something you are describing or saying, but rhyme is not essential.

In the poem 'Remember?', the poet uses rhyming couplets:
Remember the days? Now think back hard
To the time when the loo was down the yard.

This rhyme works well in the poem because it suits the topic, memories of childhood.

In a 'Child's supper' the poet uses rhyme as well but not so regularly:
A cold mother. A harsh father
Their legs are under the table
The lino is pretty with roses bright red
But you can't pick them. The flowers are dead.
Under the table there isn't a sound
And nothing, nothing at all goes round.

Use rhyme in your own poems when you think it performs a definite purpose in the poem, but do *not* use rhyme mechanically just because you think poetry ought to rhyme.

■ Writer's workshop 2 ■
Free verse

The shape or form of some poems is dictated by what the poet wants to say. These free-form poems or examples of free verse follow no regular pattern of verse form, lengths of lines, or rhyming pattern.

'For June' is a poem that could be described as 'free form':
We were sitting in a cafe
I remember
talking over cigarettes and wine
and suddenly . . .

There is no rhyme. The length of the lines is dictated by the content of the poem or the emotion of the verse.

The structure of the different verses alters according to what the poet wants to say within each verse.

But writing in free verse does *not* mean;
- a poem can be shapeless;
- a poem can be without rhythm;
- a poem can have no pattern.

Free verse allows the poet to find a form for the poem that suits the content; the form of the poem is therefore an extension of the content.

Suggestions for written work
Rhyme
1. Write two versions of any one of the following subjects; in the first version you should use rhyme, in the second version do not use rhyme.
   a. a poem recalling vivid sensations (sights, sounds, smells, pleasures) of your childhood.
   b. a poem about any aspect of family life (e.g. special events, quarrels, sadness, joy)
   c. a poem about a domestic pet.

Free verse

2. Write a poem in free verse about a relative, a friend or someone you admire in which you try to express what is individual about the person.

3. Write a poem in free verse about the changes you see in your area as the year passes. Give it the title 'The Four Seasons'.

Poetry and the community

Poetry can deal with almost any subject or theme. Poems do not need to be about nature, beauty, descriptions of the countryside or love.

The four poems, 'Carnival', 'Kurtin up at Ra Barras', 'The street's gossip' and 'Job Centre' have as their subjects:

a street festival;

a large open-air market in Glasgow;

a local character;

a place where people see what jobs are available.

These are everyday places, ordinary people and events.

■ **Writer's workshop 3** ■
Imagery

Imagery is the word used to describe language in poems that appeals to our senses: sight, sound, touch, smell, movement.

By imagery, the poet tries to convey a picture to the reader that captures in words the essential things about the things he is writing about, for example in 'Job Centre' the poet uses this imagery: "The place is as bright as lipstick' and 'A staccato of neat white cards'.

This imagery uses direct comparisons ('bright as lipstick') and indirect comparisons ('staccato of neat white cards'), where the qualities associated with the word 'staccato' are given to the cards. Elsewhere in the poem, the poet uses literal images as symbols to express what she wants to convey about the job centre: 'a label tied round a cold big toe'; 'That's me – a card in a drawer'. A lot of the impact of poems comes from the imagery a poet uses. In your own poems try to find images that express what you want to say.

Suggestions for written work

Write poems about any of the following places in your area. You may choose to write in a local dialect if you wish. Try to express something important about the places in the imagery you use:
  a local market;
  an annual celebration or festival;
  a well-known local character;
  your local park;
  your school;
  the local football or sports stadium;
  any local landmark.

Poetry and social issues

'Yesterday, today and tomorrow', 'To you, woman of South Africa' and 'Distant sounds' all have something to say about what is going on in the world. Poetry can deal with public issues and topical questions, and poets can choose to make their own position on the issue clear to the reader.

Suggestions for written work

1. Write a poem with one of these titles:
    'What I believe';
    'What I fear';
    'The years ahead';
2. Write a poem about any issue (social, political, personal) about which you care deeply.

Further reading

ed Benton	*Touchstones* (Hodder)
ed Cosman Keefe and Wearer	*Penguin Book of Women Poets*
ed J. Couzyn	*The Bloodaxe Book of Contemporary Women Poets* (Bloodaxe Books)
ed Crang	*Tunes on a Whistle* (Arnold-Wheaton)
ed Heaney and Hughes	*The Rattle Bag* (Faber)
ed Hidden	*Many People, Many Voices* (Hutchinson)
ed Gardner	*Up the Line to Death* (Eyre Methuen)
ed Larkin	*The Oxford Book of 20th Century Verse*
ed Rhodri Jones	*One World Poets* (Heinemann)

Thomas Nelson and Sons Ltd
Nelson House Mayfield Road
Walton-on-Thames Surrey
KT12 5PL UK

51 York Place
Edinburgh
EH1 3JD UK

Thomas Nelson (Hong Kong) Ltd
Toppan Building 10/F
22A Westlands Road
Quarry Bay Hong Kong

Distributed in Australia by

Thomas Nelson Australia
480 La Trobe Street
Melbourne Victoria 3000
and in Sydney, Brisbane, Adelaide and Perth

© Don Shiach 1987

First published by Thomas Nelson and Sons Ltd 1987
ISBN 0–17–432172–4
NPN: 01
Printed in Great Britain by M. & A. Thomson Litho Ltd.

Acknowledgements
The author and publishers are grateful to the following for permission to reproduce
copyright material:
Birmingham Branch of NATE for 'Jack at the Palace' by Chris Flanagan from
Birmingham Voices; Centerprise Trust Ltd for 'The Rest is History' by Sue May from
Where's there's smoke, 'A Visitor' by Ellen Richardson from *Writing*, 'For June' by
Billie Hunter from *Some Grit, Some Fire* and 'When you don't feel like a stranger'
by Rita from *Breaking the Silence*; Commonword Ltd for 'Carnival' by Kevin Otoo and
'Letting Go' by Bernadette Tweedale from *Write on*; The Gatehouse Project for 'The
Street's Gossip' by Mary Whittaker from *Yes I Like it*; Green Ink Writers for 'A Man
like Mulloy' by Michael Hannon from *Over here, Over there*; Heeley Writers for 'D
for Dad' by Beth Edge from *Down to Heel*; Tyneside Writers Workshop for 'For Women
of South Africa' by Anneliese Klock from *Bells Caught*; Yorkshire Art Circus Ltd for
'Glassworks' by Fred Taylor and 'Sweetmaking' by Nellie Oldroyd from *All in a Day's
Work*; Your Own Stuff Press for 'Satch' by Gordon Clay and 'Jimmy takes the Lead'
by Pete Hannah from *Egypt Road to Cairo Street*.
We are unable to trace the copyright holders of some of the material used in this
anthology and would appreciate any information which would enable us to do so.
Photographs: p.3 Harris Museum and Art Gallery (Preston); p.6 Homer Sykes;
p.10 Chris Steele-Perkins; pp.25, 28 Thomas Nelson and Sons Ltd; p.31 Steve
Boon; pp.35, 37 Thomas Nelson and Sons Ltd; p.40 David Simson; p.42 Anthony
Hayes; p.72 BBC Hulton Picture Library; p.103 Thomas Nelson and Sons Ltd; p.107
Shelter; pp.111, 113 Anthony Hayes; p.119 Thomas Nelson and Sons Ltd; *cover*
Impact Photos.
Text edited by Mandy Green